First Workshop on Storytelling 2018

New Orleans, Louisiana, USA
5 June 2018

ISBN: 978-1-5108-6365-1

NAACL HLT 2018

Storytelling

Proceedings of the First Workshop

June 5, 2018
New Orleans, Louisiana

Google

Introduction

Welcome to the first *ACL workshop on Storytelling!

Human storytelling has existed for as far back as we can trace, predating writing. Humans have used stories for entertainment, education, cultural preservation; to convey experiences, history, lessons, morals; and to share the human experience.

Part of grounding artificial intelligence work in human experience can involve the generation, understanding, and sharing of stories. This workshop highlights the diverse work being done in storytelling and AI across different fields.

Papers at this workshop are multi-disciplinary, including work on neural, pipeline, and linguistic approaches to understanding and creating stories.

We are also pleased to host a Visual Storytelling challenge, highlighting different methods for automatically generating stories given a set of images; and an invited talk from Nasrin Mostafazadeh on communicating about events through storytelling.

Enjoy the workshop!

Workshop website: `http://www.visionandlanguage.net/workshop2018`

Storytelling Challenge

The Storytelling challenge provides teams with the VIST dataset to generate stories from sequences of five images, and is hosted on EvalAI. Submissions for the challenge at NAACL 2018 were evaluated using both automatic metrics and human evaluation. The winner was chosen based on the best performance across the human evaluations for **focus**, **structure and coherence**, **detail**, how **visually grounded** the stories were, how **shareable** the stories were, and whether they sounded like they were **written by a human**. More details can be found on the workshop website.

Submissions came from the following teams all over the world.

DG-DLMX
Diana González-Rico, Gibran Fuentes-Pineda
Institute for Research in Applied Mathematics and Systems (IIMAS), Universidad Nacional Autónoma de México (UNAM)

NLPSA 501
Chao-Chun Hsu, Szu-Min Chen, Ming-Hsun Hsieh, Lun-Wei Ku
Academia Sinica, Taiwan

UCSB-NLP
Xin Wang, Wenhu Chen, Yuan-Fang Wang, and William Yang Wang
University of California, Santa Barbara, USA

SnuBiVtt
Min-Oh Heo, Taehyeong Kim, Kyung-Wha Park, Seonil Son, Byoung-Tak Zhang
Seoul National University

More details on the systems and winning team will be provided at the workshop, and made available on the website after the workshop!

Challenge website: http://www.visionandlanguage.net/workshop2018/#challenge

Organizers:

Margaret Mitchell, Google Research
Ting-Hao 'Kenneth' Huang, Carnegie Mellon University
Francis Ferraro, University of Maryland, Baltimore County
Ishan Misra, Carnegie Mellon University

Program Committee:

Elizabeth Clark
David Elson
Marjan Ghazvininejad
Andrew Gordon
Gunhee Kim
Boyang Li
Stephanie Lukin
Joao Magalhaes
Lara Martin
Saif Mohammad
Nasrin Mostafazadeh
Mark Riedl
Luowei Zhou

Invited Speaker:

Nasrin Mostafazadeh, Elemental Cognition

Event-centric Context Modeling:
The Case of Story Comprehension and Story Generation

Building AI systems that can process natural language input, comprehend it, and generate an engaging and contextually relevant output in response, has been one of the longest-running goals in AI. In human-human communications, a major trigger to our meaningful communications are "events" and how they cause/enable future events. We often communicate through telling stories in the form of related series of events.

In this talk, I present my work on language processing in terms of events and how they interact with each other in time. Mainly through the lens of storytelling, I will focus on story comprehension and collaborative story generation, with a major emphasis on commonsense reasoning and narrative knowledge as showcased in the Story Cloze Test framework. Through different use cases, I will highlight the importance of establishing a contentful context and modeling multimodal contexts (such as visual and textual) in various AI tasks.

Table of Contents

Conference Program

Tuesday, June 5, 2018

10:00–10:10   ***Opening Remarks***

10:15–11:00   *Invited Talk by Nasrin Mostafazedeh*

11:00–11:25   *Learning to Listen: Critically Considering the Role of AI in Human Storytelling and Character Creation*
Anna Kasunic and Geoff Kaufman

11:25–11:50   *Linguistic Features of Helpfulness in Automated Support for Creative Writing*
Melissa Roemmele and Andrew Gordon

11:50–13:45   ***Lunch***

13:45–14:10   *A Pipeline for Creative Visual Storytelling*
Stephanie Lukin, Reginald Hobbs and Clare Voss

14:10–14:35   *Telling Stories with Soundtracks: An Empirical Analysis of Music in Film*
Jon Gillick and David Bamman

14:35–15:00   *Towards Controllable Story Generation*
Nanyun Peng, Marjan Ghazvininejad, Jonathan May and Kevin Knight

15:00–15:20   ***Break***

15:20–16:00   *Storytelling Challenge*

16:00–16:25   *An Encoder-decoder Approach to Predicting Causal Relations in Stories*
Melissa Roemmele and Andrew Gordon

16:25–16:50   *Neural Event Extraction from Movies Description*
Alex Tozzo, Dejan Jovanovic and Mohamed Amer

Learning to Listen: Critically Considering the Role of AI in Human Storytelling and Character Creation

Anna Kasunic
Carnegie Mellon University
Human-Computer Interaction Institute
Pittsburgh, PA USA
akasunic@andrew.cmu.edu

Geoff Kaufman
Carnegie Mellon University
Human-Computer Interaction Institute
Pittsburgh, PA USA
gfk@cs.cmu.edu

Abstract

In this opinion piece, we argue that there is a need for alternative design directions to complement existing AI efforts in narrative and character generation and algorithm development. To make our argument, we a) outline the predominant roles and goals of AI research in storytelling; b) present existing discourse on the benefits and harms of narratives; and c) highlight the pain points in character creation revealed by semi-structured interviews we conducted with 14 individuals deeply involved in some form of character creation. We conclude by proffering several specific design avenues that we believe can seed fruitful research collaborations. In our vision, AI collaborates with humans during creative processes and narrative generation, helps amplify voices and perspectives that are currently marginalized or misrepresented, and engenders experiences of narrative that support spectatorship and listening roles.

1 Introduction

> Somebody gets into trouble. Gets out of it again. People *love* that story!
> (Vonnegut, 1970)

Once upon a time, people decided it was not enough to share stories; as humans are as much a curious animal as we are a storytelling one, we sought to study them. Theories of narratology, or the study or narratives, defines and breaks down narratives according to their distinct states of action, events, and elements (Prince, 1974; Bal, 2009) and (for the most part) narratologists agree that to constitute a narrative, a text must tell a story, exist in a world, be situated in time, include intelligent agents, and have some form of causal chain of events. Narratives also usually seeks to convey something meaningful to an audience (Ryan et al., 2007). (Note: In this paper, we are somewhat relaxed with the terms "story" and "narrative," and will often use the two interchangeably). With the advancement of artificial intelligence (AI), research related to narratives has taken on a whole new shape and meaning; not only are there new narrative forms ripe for the studying, including more examples of stories that are interactive and branching (Ryan and Rebreyend, 2013), but there is also a whole field of research devoted to improving AI storytelling capabilities.

Although research that teaches AI to tell better stories is challenging and intriguing on many levels, research and discourse in domains like psychology, literary fiction, and even social media suggests that a) humans benefit from telling stories, so AI might serve us better if it nurtures our storytelling predilections rather than act solely as storyteller, and that b) after all these years, we as humans still have a lot to learn and improve when it comes to telling narratives. Our stories brim with issues of representation, bias, and authenticity that can dilute or negate the beneficial powers of consuming and interacting with narratives, and our social structures promote certain stories while silencing others. If we're not careful, AI storytellers will only inherit and exacerbate these problematic patterns. In what follows, we present an opinion piece that urges researchers at the intersections of AI, natural language processing (NLP), human-computer interaction (HCI), and storytelling to envision different futures for research related to AI and storytelling. In this paper, to be clear, we do not strive to present precise quantitative or qualitative conclusions or recommendations, nor are we exhaustive in our presentation of extant storytelling research, discourse, and innovations. Rather, we seek to spark dialogues, questions, and cross-discipline exchanges around the role of AI in storytelling. To this end, we discuss existing conversations and

Proceedings of the First Workshop on Storytelling, pages 1–13
New Orleans, Louisiana, June 5, 2018. ©2018 Association for Computational Linguistics

research from human-computer interaction, AI, and other domains concerned with storytelling; we provide anecdotal highlights from interviews we conducted with character creators; and we illuminate alternative, promising directions for AI storytelling research. We begin by outlining some of the predominant roles that AI research in storytelling has held in order to provide context for our discussion. As a framing note, readers should be aware that we will use the term AI to encompass different forms of computational approaches that may not fall within everyone's defined scope of AI. Whatever their specific disciplines or perspectives, we humbly request that our readers relax their definitions of AI for the duration of this paper to include computational approaches, more broadly.

2 Predominant Roles of AI in Narratives

We can categorize AI work in storytelling in three ways: 1) teaching AI to generate and understand stories; 2) helping human storytellers as a co-creator; and 3) modeling story elements. Some of the earliest work in storytelling and AI focused on improving AI's understanding of stories using scripts, or "boring little stories" in the words of the authors (Schank et al., 1975; Schank and Abelson, 1975). As technology advanced, more research attention shifted to using AI to generate stories. For example, the hypertext fiction model emerged, in which links to branching narratives allowed for branching stories and some level of direct agency over the story (Bolter and Joyce, 1987). Researchers have continued making advances in story generation, developing AI story, world, and character generators that are planning- or event-sequence-based (Fairclough and Cunningham, 2004; Lebowitz, 1987; Porteous and Cavazza, 2009; Riedl and Young, 2010; Young et al., 2004; Barber and Kudenko, 2007; Min et al., 2008). Generators may also be character-centric, in which players' interactions with intelligent agents move the stories forward (Magerko, 2006; Swartjes and Theune, 2006; Cavazza et al., 2002). This work most commonly aims to create entertainment value, with an emphasis on learning and catering to player preferences (e.g., (Thue et al., 2007)) and is often framed in terms of applications to interactive narratives, even if the potential applications of the work could extend to narratives, in general.

However, the goals of AI research in narratives are not exclusively focused on AI story generation; some work also strives to teach machines how to be more "human" through stories (Huang et al., 2016; Riedl and Harrison, 2016). Although much less common, some prior work has also positioned AI as co-creator, encouraging and guiding humans in creating their own stories (Ryokai and Cassell, 1999; Bers and Cassell, 1998; Van Broeckhoven et al., 2015). We have also seen work in the interactive drama space in which human-allowed actions are more open-ended, positioning humans to act more like actors on a stage than characters that must conform to a limited story world (Mateas and Stern, 2003). In addition, some research in modeling stories has focused not on story generation, but on understanding (and subsequently improving) human experiences of narratives. For example, work in identifying "emotional arcs" looks at mood shifts and audience engagement in experiencing narratives (Chu and Roy, 2017; Reagan, 2017), and other work has endeavored to identify turning points in stories (Ouyang and McKeown, 2015), model the shapes of stories (Mani, 2012; Elson, 2012), and understand the relationships of characters to narrative arcs (Bamman et al., 2014b,a). These works have identified what people enjoy about stories, have learned from our existing stories, and subsequently can augment story generation efforts.

In short, for the (many) story-lovers among us, it's an exciting time to be working in AI, NLP and HCI. However, as we will discuss in the next section, there can be potential dangers in placing AI in a storytelling role, in aligning AI storytelling research too closely with interactive narratives, and in catering too much to the preferences of the humans engaging in stories and games. We now to turn to a discussion of both the benefits and potential harms of storytelling as they relate to extant work on AI in narratives.

3 The Pleasures and Perils of Narratives

3.1 The Complex Pleasures of Narrative

Scholars in philosophy, psychology, anthropology, and related disciplines have characterized storytelling as fundamental to how we as humans grow, learn, develop, and process and experience the world, (Jung, 1964; Dautenhahn and Nehaniv, 1998; Sutton-Smith, 1986, 2012; Paley, 2009; Cooper, 1993). As such, our desire to engage in stories and storytelling is not a "frivolous impulse, but a fundamental adaptive response" (Rose, 2012). As an experimental study from the 1940s has shown, we go so far as to ascribe narrative to situations where no narrative form exists (Heider and Simmel, 1944). Although AI research in emotional arcs recommends "happy" endings and seeks to maximize positive moods (Chu and Roy, 2017; Reagan, 2017), other research suggests that the relationship between story enjoyment and emotion is more complex. Research on benign masochism tells us that the human brain can derive pleasure from negative reactions and feelings such as sadness, fear, and disgust (Rozin et al., 2013). For example, sad films can be highly enjoyable, especially for certain groups such as female and younger viewers (Oliver, 1993, 2003; Mares et al., 2008). Similarly, research has found that mixed emotional experiences, such as experiencing both happiness and sadness rather than just one or the other, can be beneficial to one's physical health (Hershfield et al., 2013). Thus, AI work that focuses on maximizing human enjoyment may overemphasize "sunny" experiences of narratives, and by focusing on pleasure rather than growth, may favor stories with narratives that fail to challenge and aid in human development.

Entertainment through narratives can be a valuable end goal in itself, but it can also have other, attendant advantages. According to transportation theory, we can achieve immersion in narrative worlds through identification with characters and perceptions of plausibility or the "suspension of disbelief," in which we view narrative worlds and character actions as authentic (Green et al., 2004, 2003; Tesser et al., 2005). Not only does this transportation lead to enjoyment, but it can also enable perspective taking and belief change, (Kaufman and Libby, 2012; Berns et al., 2013). It can positively transform us, e.g. leading us to personality growth and maturation (Djikic et al., 2009b), with potentially higher transformative effects on attitudes for those who are resistant to change, or have diminished emotionality (Dal Cin et al., 2004; Djikic et al., 2009a). Reading fiction has been shown to improve the ability to attribute mental states to oneself and others (known as Theory of Mind), an important cognitive foundation for complex social relationships (Kidd and Castano, 2013), and reading narratives can lead us to feel psychologically connected to groups of characters, increasing feel-

ings of belongingness and subsequently leading to greater feelings of satisfaction and more positive mood (Gabriel and Young, 2011).

3.2 On "Listening" Versus "Agentic" Narrative Forms

The jury is still out, however, on which forms of media provoke higher levels of transportation, transformation, and enjoyment. Here, we find it useful to separate "listening" forms of narrative from "agentic" forms of narrative, and we will use these terms throughout the remaineder of the paper. We characterize "listening" narratives as positioning the consumer of the narrative in a more passive role, listening or watching the story rather than making direct decisions that define or shape the characters, the plot, or the narrative world. "Listening" narratives would include traditional, typically non-branching narratives such as films, novels, and short stories. We define "agentic" narratives as stories in which the narrative consumer has some level of direct agency over characters, plot, or other story elements. In our definition, "agentic" narratives are akin to interactive narratives, and this aligns with other definitions of interactive narratives. For example, agency in the context of interactive narratives can be said to occur when the world "responds expressively and coherently to our engagement with it" (Murray, 2004). Accordingly, we prefer to stress the idea of agency over interaction because we do not think that "listening" narratives preclude interaction. Indeed, other researchers and designers ostensibly share our view of agency in narratives as nebulously interactive. For example, Persausive Games has produced experiences that question the notion of how much traditional game definitions of agency truly allows players to interact with and engage in a narrative (Bogost, 2005, 2006), and other researchers have chosen to use the term "agency play" rather than agency to suggest that interactive narratives require more expansive notions of interactivity (Harrell and Zhu, 2009). As we consider the future of narrative expression and consumption, we can consider the possibility of listening narratives that allow narrative consumers to interact without directly making decisions about narrative or character arcs and shapes.

Indeed, studies have found that traditional "listening" forms such as books and movies may be equally or even more engaging and transformational than "agentic" narratives (Oh et al., 2014; Green et al., 2008; Jenkins, 2014). However, other studies have found that enjoyment and identification can be higher in agentic narratives (Hefner et al., 2007; Elson et al., 2014; Hand and Varan, 2008). It may also be that certain types of interaction may have varying costs and benefits. For example, a study allowing for character customization actually decreased narrative engagement and enjoyment, showing that the qualities of a narrative, not character agency, might be more important (Green et al., 2004).

We make no attempt to argue for "listening" over "agentic" forms of engagement with narratives, but we do believe that listening forms warrant more attention. For example, advancements in AI mechanisms for branching narratives needn't apply to exclusively agentic forms of narrative; we can also think in terms of new listening experiences that are simultaneously branching and non-agentic (listening). A large body of work on branching narratives could be translated into new forms of listening rather than agentic digital media; for example, researchers have shown how their work in story generation techniques like plot graphs can be applied to branching (not necessarily agentic) narratives (Li et al., 2013; Guzdial et al., 2015). However, to our knowledge, there does not exist a wide range of practical applications of advancements in story generation and branching narrative work to new, listening forms of narrative.

Some analogies may be useful here. In describing his affinity for both traditional (listening) and interactive (agentic) narratives, storyteller and SIMS creator Will Wright likens traditional narratives to a roller coaster, and games and interactive narratives to a dirt bike (Rose, 2012). Neither experience is necessarily "better" than the other; whether the driver or the passenger, each has their unique benefits and affordances. Moreover, just as the invention of the roller coaster enabled new forms of "riding", listening forms of narrative needn't necessarily be "traditional." Just as humans enjoy, learn, and develop through social interaction, we also have much to gain by spectatorship such as the popular pastime of "people-watching." Just as there is value in active thinking, there is also value in meditating (watching our thoughts pass by without directly engaging). We argue that by focusing so much scholarly attention on agentic forms of narrative, we may be missing out on ways to use technology to engender new ways of listening. Technological advancements in branching narratives, for example, could be realized by means of listening narratives rather than agentic narratives; we can consider the potential benefits of narratives that allow a multitude of experiences and paths, without conceding choice or agency to the listener/spectator.

Lastly, although existing efforts in AI narrative generation would suggest that humans benefit primarily from the experience of receiving narratives, the *telling* of stories can be highly beneficial. They can help us develop resilience, (East et al., 2010), provide therapeutic benefits (Block and Leseho, 2005; Carlick and Biley, 2004; Chelf et al., 2000; Pennebaker, 1997), and activate imaginative processes that are key to human growth and development (Harris, 2000). Thus, as with the narrowness of focus on interactive (agentic) rather than listening forms of narrative, prioritizing AI's role as storyteller misses valuable opportunities for empowering humans as storytellers.

3.3 The Potential Harms of Existing Narratives

In addition, as we consider AI-enhanced storytelling experiences, we need to be mindful that our starting points— the story frames that we use to train AI— may unintentionally marginalize, misrepresent, and altogether exclude many groups. Just as recent work in natural language processing has criticized and sought ways to rectify the amplification of negative biases (e.g. gender biases) in NLP techniques (Dwork et al., 2012; Zhao et al., 2017; Bolukbasi et al., 2016; Voigt et al., 2017), AI storytelling has the potential to amplify and exacerbate issues of bias and diversity, which in turn excludes certain individuals from experiencing the potential benefits of story engagement. For example, AI story generators that learn from existing narrative corpora may learn that straight white male characters are best suited to be protagonists or figures of power, and that genderqueer and people of color should occupy sidekick roles. These stereotypes may persist regardless of the identification of the human author; for example, a study of online fan-fiction found that gendered stereotypes were highly common, and perpetuated by both male and female-identifying authors (Fast et al., 2016). Thus, machine learning models may also learn from patterns of speech and role characterizations that stereotype certain groups, decreasing character authenticity. This is especially worrisome because research demonstrates that narrative persuasion is less effective if people cannot identify with the characters (So and Nabi, 2013; Ritterfeld and Jin, 2006; Slater et al., 2006; Gillig and Murphy, 2016).

Many popular films fail the classic Bechdel test, which simply specifies that the movie must 1) feature at least two women, 2) that these women must talk to each other, and 3) that their conversation must concern something other than a man (Selisker, 2015), and fare even worse on new NLP techniques that assess power differentials between men and women in movies (Sap et al., 2017). Issues of representation in film highlighted by the 2014 and 2015 Oscars, in which all awardees were white, sparked a social media firestorm under the hashtag #OscarsSoWhite (Syed, 2016; Borum Chattoo, 2018), and brought to further light a history of under-representation in film, with only 6.4% of all awardees since 1929 (1,688) being non-white (Berman, 2016). Minority groups are often under-, mis-, or negatively represented in film and other forms of narrative (Okoye, 2016; Smith, 2009; Hooks et al., 2006). In writing communities, gendered violence under the dominance of a "straight male cisgender patriarchy" and exclusion of black and brown writers from major literary publications has spawned a wave of debate and protest about exclusion, marginalization, and the silencing of voices (Tsay et al., 2015; Groom, 2015). Such issues suggest that AI may be more useful to us as an aid that can help identify biases and stereotypes, and amplify muffled voices, rather than a generator that replicates and extends our existing, problematic narratives.

In the next section, we cull anecdotal excerpts from a series of interviews we conducted with individuals deeply involved with some form of character creation to reveal existing pain points in human's attempts to avoid and address issues of biasing, stereotyping, under-representation, and misrepresentation. Our interviewees' discussions suggest concrete, specific ways in which AI can aid humans in improving some of the more problematic elements of our existing storytelling efforts.

4 An Exploration of Challenges in Character Creation

> The one thing about being a dude and writing from a female perspective is that the baseline is, you suck.

As author Junot Díaz's quote above (Rosenberg, 2012) points out, creating characters can be an intractable challenge. Unless we are in the rare case of writing a story that is only about the self, with no secondary characters, creating the "Other"— a character who is different from oneself along one or multiple dimensions (Shawl and Ward, 2005)— is inevitable. As humans, we define ourselves along multiple axes of identity, including gender, sexuality, race/ethnicity, class, nationality, health, disability, education, and passions/interests, to name a few; some axes may be especially salient for some individuals, and inconsequential for others. We posit that anxiety and uncertainty about how to authentically and sensitively create characters who are Other can hinder both the creative process and the narrative experience, as inauthentic characters can also impede character identification and subsequent narrative transportation and enjoyment. Understanding the ways in which human character creators approach and grapple with creating characters that are Other can provide insights into where the most crucial needs lie, and how we might design AI systems to assist with rather than model human stories. To this end, we conducted interviews to explore and better understand the space of character creation and its attendant pain points. Below, we present anecdotal highlights of interviews as they pertain to insights into needs for assistive AI; a full presentation of our methodology and qualitative analysis processes can be found elsewhere (more information available upon request).

We conducted qualitative, semi-structured interviews with 14 individuals with deep involvement in character creation, including novelists, short story writers, poets, journalists, television and game writers, actors, directors, and role-playing gamers, game masters, and designers (including both tabletop and live-action role-playing games). These character creators, recruited with the help of professors in relevant departments at our local university, ranged in age from 19 to 62 (average of 45), and held education levels from "some college" to PhD. All spoke English as a primary language, and primarily were born and raised in the U.S. Eight identified as male, five as female, and one as non-binary; 11/14 identified as white, one as black, one as Native American, and one as Asian. For several of our participants, aspects of the narrative creation process constituted their full-time occupation or activity—e.g. writer, videographer, professor of drama or literature, and game designer— whereas others pursued narrative and/or character creation as a passion, hobby or pastime while also holding another occupation, such as secretary, civil servant, human resources coordinator, or student. With IRB approval, we audio-recorded the interviews (each lasting roughly 40-70 minutes), transcribed, and qualitatively analyzed using open-coding techniques to identify patterns across our participants.

We asked our participants to describe their processes of creating or embodying their characters, what informs the development of their characters, on what axes they identify with or diverge from their characters, and what conflicts or hesitations they have in creating or embodying certain kinds of characters. These responses validated existing research on the benefits of storytelling as a source of joy and growth. As one participant put it, "you get shaped by these stories that touch you, and by the sources that touch you. And I think you develop greater empathy. I think you become a better human being though that" (p2). The results of our interviews offer key insights about how AI systems can support humans in character creation and storytelling efforts, which we can organize into three themes: 1) the distinct ways in which different participants struggled and dealt with inauthenticity concerns; 2) the pain points participants discussed about giving voice to characters from under-represented groups; and 3) the impact of collaboration on character creation.

4.1 Concerns about Inauthentic Characters

Our participants generally fell into one of two camps when it came to relationships between their characters and their self-identity. Either a) they specifically chose characters they viewed as similar to themselves, operating under the adage, "write what you know" or b) they grounded themselves in notions of universality, seeking to find elements of themselves in characters that were seemingly highly divergent from themselves. Yet both groups expressed feelings of discomfort with

and anxiety about representing different viewpoints, suggesting opportunities for AI to assist with authentic character representation.

Participants that fell into group A explained that certain character decisions were outside their comfort zones, e.g. role-playing a character of an opposite gender (p9, p12). Another participant stated, "I'm very careful about running mental illnesses that I don't and have never have. Because I'm sensitive enough to portrayals of my own, that I kind of don't want to screw that up." (p13). Other participants echoed this sentiment of certain stories or portrayals being "not my story to tell" (p4).

Participants in group B felt it was very important to include diverse characters in their stories and games in order to be more inclusive, but many of these participants expressed concern that despite their best efforts, they might be misrepresenting characters that identified in ways differently from themselves. They wanted to remain inside the lines of what they felt, as one participant worded it, "cultural appreciation" rather than "cultural appropriation" (p9). One role-player was initially hesitant to move outside her own identity. She had slowly branched into different ethnicities, genders, and sexualities, but had lingering apprehension regarding whether her portrayals were ethical and authentic, saying "Hopefully I'm not being horribly insulting to anyone of that ethnicity or sexuality while playing them. I hope I'm not. I think I'm not. I think I'm doing it relatively sensitively (p11). Thus, AI could be helpful in flagging characters that might be cause for concern by perpetuating certain stereotypes or offenses.

4.2 Issues of Representation

We have given examples in this paper of narrative exclusion along lines of gender and race/ethnicity; concerns related to these topic arose often in our interviews, and suggests opportunities for AI to offer additional support. For example, one of our participants, a drama director, said he made a purposeful decision to cast racially diverse actors in his plays (p3).

Yet even among those for whom improving the representation of certain under-represented groups is a priority, there can be conflict over *how* we should represent such groups. For example, one participant (p1) spoke of the controversies in TV writing communities around what it means to write authentic characters of color. He spoke of a panel he participated in about TV representations of people of color in which many of the panelists were sharply divided on the questions: Is it okay for a character to be universal in identity, such that someone of a different race could conceivably play that character? Or ought characters be steeped in the specifics of their social identities and contexts? Participants also brought up issues of exclusion along axes that are often overlooked. For example, one participant discussed issues with neurotypical privilege, explaining that collaborative storytelling games are often exclusionary because they require players to pool from a relatively common pool of narrative tropes, meanings and interpretations that are not easy accessible to those who are neurodivergent (p8). These concerns about and disagreements on how to authentically and sensitively represent different groups indicate that AI that could serve to assist humans in grappling with and reflecting on these issues.

4.3 Impact of Collaboration on Character Creation

Where writers of novels or short stories may be more likely to develop narratives relatively autonomously and in isolation, other media lend themselves to highly collaborative environments, such as role-playing games (where the game master and the role-playing actors interact to shape the narrative), writing for the stage or screen (where writers interface with actors that embody their characters), and video game writing (where it is common for large teams to collaborate). Participants in narrative media with more collaborative development processes spoke enthusiastically of how actors and other characters had reshaped their understandings of their own characters. For example, a participant who is a playwright discussed how interactions with actors often reshaped not just a character, but a whole play (p4). Similarly, a screenwriter-participant (p7) discussed completely revising a major scene after an actress revealed she couldn't "in her wildest dreams" imagine taking the action assigned to her. The interviewee stated that he often gains invaluable insights from actors, and explained that the relationship between actors and their characters are symbiotic; if an actor can't feel they can be true to a character, then everything will fall apart. Role players and game masters spoke of how interactions with other characters shaped their understandings of their own characters, and affected the decisions they made in the game. Where writers in less collaborative contexts do research and seek guidance from those they feel may have more expertise or insight, in these more collaborative contexts, characters are not just created; they are constantly negotiated and re-negotiated. Through these processes of negotiation, our participants explained that they felt their characters took on more authentic, lifelike forms. However, not all narrative media are structured to automatically support such forms of collaboration and feedback, and not all narrators and character creators have access to social circles that can enable such collaboration. Intelligent agents that can play similar roles to human collaborators (e.g., other role players and actors) could provide critical, transformative feedback to creators and narrativists that work in relative isolation.

In sum, our interviews indicate that AI could be helpful as a storytelling assistant or co-creator by offering practical assistance (e.g. flagging misrepresentations), providing support for reflection on representation, and by taking on character embodiment roles that are usually assumed by humans in collaborative creation contexts.

5 Discussion

As we move forward towards new forms of media, narrative, and interaction, we urge scholars to take a step back and question the *whys* of AI in storytelling. Based on existing research and current trends in AI and other domains invested in narratives, and informed by the qualitative interviews our team conducted with character creators, we recommend a reorientation towards how we conceptualize the role of AI in storytelling. Yes, we can keep moving towards a future in which AI becomes more and more adept at human forms of storytelling. But is that the preferred future? As we consider the joys and benefits humans experience by engaging in storytelling, the shortcomings of our current narrative forms and processes that can exclude groups and dilute the transformative power of narratives, and both the struggles and affordances of different processes of character creation, we see several potential branches that future AI narrative systems can grow. Here, we return to the idea of "listening": we envision AI that better listens to human storytellers and assists us as co-creators, and AI-assisted narrative forms that enable "listening" rather than "agentic" engagement. We give examples of specific starting ideas we have for 1) designing AI to support human storytellers, and 2) investigating "listening" rather than "agentic" forms of narrative that we hope will inspire the growth of new branches of AI narrative research. We acknowledge that the current state of computational powers renders some of our suggestions only feasible through at least partial Wizard of Oz approaches; we consider these ideas as starting points to guide future research and scientific advancements. Although we think current paths of AI research merit continued work and investigation, we believe that these alternate paths of inquiry and design are at least equally promising and important.

5.1 AI and Crowd-Powered Feedback Mechanisms for Human Storytellers

As we saw from our literature review and our interviews, humans *enjoy* storytelling; they grow, learn, and heal from it. However, as we saw in our interviews, creating authentic characters can be a challenging and emotionally fraught task, and as we saw from discussions of (mis)representation and stereotyping in film and literature, the stories that humans currently create are not the ideal models for AI to emulate. Thus, instead of expending all our effort on teaching AI to tell stories, we can divert some of our energies to using AI to help humans tell the stories they may struggle to tell. AI has already been used to model emotional arcs in narrative, and to identify bias in a number of domains. AI could be leveraged to better identify potential problems that could dilute authenticity and stymie narrative transportation, such as exclusion and stereotyping. There are a number of approaches that already use crowd-powered "mini-corpora" to teach AI how to generate narrative, (Guzdial et al., 2015; Li et al., 2012, 2013, 2014; Purdy and Riedl, 2016) but this existing work does not seek to improve experiences or engage crowd-workers in meaningful forms of storytelling. Taking cues from work in improving crowd workers experiences by inducing curiosity (Law et al., 2016), we might further consider crowd-powered feedback mechanisms could allow both story creators and crowd workers to engage in and benefit from stories in different ways.

For example, taking a character-centric approach, AI systems could prove useful in identifying when characters begin to fall into traps of stereotypes or implausibility. We could consider training models using a combination of existing corpora and crowdsourcing; as a secondary benefit, we could design crowdsourcing studies such that they engage crowd workers in meaningful storytelling that contributes to larger, concretized goals so that crowd workers are also benefiting by consuming and ultimately contributing to revisions of narratives. Studies could invite participation from those who most identify with marginalized and underrepresented populations, and are thereby able to speak to concepts of authenticity around specific identities (including axes of identity that our interview participants highlighted, such as mental illness and neurodivergence). We could then apply these models to new narratives and use them to generate feedback for narrative creators (e.g., flagging certain depictions that are deemed to be inauthentic or insensitive); AI systems provide prompts and exercises to encourage reflective or creative practices to psychologically and creatively grapple with these challenges.

Considering the dynamics of collaborative character creation processes in domains like role playing games and acting, there could be opportunities to re-purpose advances we've made in intelligent agents. During the narrative and character creation processes, creators could engage with intelligent agents that take on certain roles in the story, and give feedback on elements that feel inauthentic or incohesive. For creators that work in relative isolation, AI could simulate the more collaborative creative atmospheres native to role-playing and acting environments, in which characters can quite literally talk back and generate thoughts of their own, thereby re-shifting and re-shaping aspects of the characters and of narratives as a whole. Under such a scenario, humans would still be the primary storytellers, just as playwrights are still the people writing the script even if they decide to make revisions and edits based on feedback they receive from actors. Although AI cannot yet simulate human intelligence to the degree that such ideas would require, we can think of ways we could use crowdsourcing and/or partial Wizard of Oz approaches to achieve similar ends and provide guidance for future goals of AI.

5.2 Innovating and Exploring "Listening" Narrative Forms

Technological progress has spawned innovation in the field of interactive narratives and narrative games, particularly in the realm of video games. However, we argue that the scholarly energy around interactive narratives might be occluding potential for technological innovation in "listening" forms of narrative in which consumers are watchers or spectators rather than active agents in the narrative. As discussed previously, research has shown that both interactive and "traditional" narrative media have positive impacts, and under certain circumstances, "traditional" narratives may be even more effective for producing particular outcomes, such as narrative transportation. However, there is room to explore what "non-traditional" listening narratives could look like and produce.

As a starting point to this path of inquiry, we could leverage existing NLP research in style transfer, which uses neural networks to learn stylistic elements of a corpus, and apply the style schema onto new texts (Kabbara and Cheung, 2016; Shen et al., 2017; Carlson et al., 2017; Fu et al., 2017; Han et al., 2017). Narratives that seek to persuade, shift opinions, or otherwise transform readers are not always successful. For example a study exposing youth to stories of LGBTQ people found that where LGBTQ youth felt more hopeful, hetero and cis youth felt more negative attitudes after the narrative exposure (Gillig and Murphy, 2016). Here, we could begin to think about how we could transform stories that could better achieve their narrative end goals (e.g., changing attitudes) in ways that better speak to different groups of readers. Automated style transfer while maintaining diegetic plausibility and coherency could be one way to achieve this, and is worth further exploring. Again, we acknowledge that given the current state of computational sophistication, such an idea would require at least partial "Wizard of Oz" approaches.

We could also think of how "listening" to AI-powered on-demand storytelling could soothe, heal, and transport in times when we cannot access human-generated stories, or in time-sensitive situations when the narrative specifications we are seeking are not readily met by existing, available stories. In the midst of a bad break-up, an episode of depression, an anxiety attack, a death of a loved one, a school or work-related failure, or any number of upsetting or traumatic experiences (potentially including the stresses of authentically representing "Other" characters in narratives), it may be difficult to reach out to others, and mustering the energy to actively engage in an agentic narrative might be too daunting. Instead, a listening form of narrative could be more helpful. An AI-powered listening narrative system could encourage certain emotional, psychological, or behavioral responses, such as allowing individuals to shift to more realistic and optimistic perspectives, or motivating individuals to reach out to friends, family or health support staff. It could be tailored to the specific situation or instance in which extra support is needed, could learn from one's engagement with other narratives to cater to personal preferences of narrative style, content, and characters, and could take various media forms, such as text, audio (including more musical or sound-oriented narratives), video, augmented reality, or virtual reality. For example, multi-modal sensing could allow for branching even in the absence of explicit listener choice, such as using the listener's nonverbal or physiological responses to make decisions or to alter the course or trajectory of the story. Given the current limitations of AI, early iterations could sample from existing corpora that have been studied to produce specific psychological or behavioral reactions.

We see these research and design suggestions as mere starting points to inspire more interesting ideas and conversations. We look forward to further discussing the opinions and ideas we've laid out in this paper, and collaborating with others who share our passions for narrative and exploring the limits and potentials of technology. In other words:

To be continued...

6 Acknowledgements

A special thanks goes to the National Science Foundation's Graduate Research Fellowship Program for their support of this work, and to Diyi Yang, Mark Riedl, Anjalie Field, Judeth Oden Choi, and all our reviewers, all of whom provided feedback, ideas, and references to literature that we earnestly but imperfectly tried to incorporate into this final version.

References

Mieke Bal. 2009. *Narratology: Introduction to the theory of narrative*. University of Toronto Press.

David Bamman, Brendan O'Connor, and Noah A Smith. 2014a. Learning latent personas of film characters. In *Proceedings of the Annual Meeting of the Association for Computational Linguistics (ACL)*, page 352.

David Bamman, Ted Underwood, and Noah A Smith. 2014b. A bayesian mixed effects model of literary character. In *Proceedings of the 52nd Annual Meeting of the Association for Computational Linguistics (Volume 1: Long Papers)*, volume 1, pages 370–379.

Heather Barber and Daniel Kudenko. 2007. A user model for the generation of dilemma-based interactive narratives. In *Workshop on Optimizing Player Satisfaction at AIIDE*, volume 7.

Eliza Berman. 2016. See the entire history of the oscars diversity problem in one chart.

Gregory S Berns, Kristina Blaine, Michael J Prietula, and Brandon E Pye. 2013. Short-and long-term effects of a novel on connectivity in the brain. *Brain connectivity*, 3(6):590–600.

Marina Umaschi Bers and Justine Cassell. 1998. Interactive storytelling systems for children: using technology to explore language and identity. *Journal of Interactive Learning Research*, 9(2):183.

Laurie Block and Johanna Leseho. 2005. listen and i tell you something: Storytelling and social action in the healing of the oppressed. *British Journal of Guidance & Counselling*, 33(2):175–184.

Ian Bogost. 2005. Airport insecurity.

Ian Bogost. 2006. Disaffected!

Jay David Bolter and Michael Joyce. 1987. Hypertext and creative writing. In *Proceedings of the ACM Conference on Hypertext*, HYPERTEXT '87, pages 41–50, New York, NY, USA. ACM.

Tolga Bolukbasi, Kai-Wei Chang, James Y Zou, Venkatesh Saligrama, and Adam T Kalai. 2016. Man is to computer programmer as woman is to homemaker? debiasing word embeddings. In *Advances in Neural Information Processing Systems*, pages 4349–4357.

Caty Borum Chattoo. 2018. Oscars so white: Gender, racial, and ethnic diversity and social issues in us documentary films (2008–2017). *Mass Communication and Society*, pages 1–27.

A Carlick and Francis C Biley. 2004. Thoughts on the therapeutic use of narrative in the promotion of coping in cancer care. *European Journal of Cancer Care*, 13(4):308–317.

Keith Carlson, Allen Riddell, and Daniel N. Rockmore. 2017. Zero-shot style transfer in text using recurrent neural networks. *CoRR*, abs/1711.04731.

Marc Cavazza, Fred Charles, and Steven J Mead. 2002. Character-based interactive storytelling. *IEEE Intelligent systems*, 17(4):17–24.

Jane Harper Chelf, Amy MB Deshler, Shauna Hillman, and Ramon Durazo-Arvizu. 2000. Storytelling: A strategy for living and coping with cancer. *Cancer Nursing*, 23(1):1–5.

Eric Chu and Deb Roy. 2017. Audio-visual sentiment analysis for learning emotional arcs in movies. *arXiv preprint arXiv:1712.02896*.

Patsy Cooper. 1993. *When Stories Come to School: Telling, Writing, and Performing Stories in the Early Childhood Classroom*. ERIC.

Sonya Dal Cin, Mark P Zanna, and Geoffrey T Fong. 2004. Narrative persuasion and overcoming resistance. *Resistance and persuasion*, pages 175–191.

Kerstin Dautenhahn and Chrystopher Nehaniv. 1998. Artificial life and natural stories. In *International Symposium on Artificial Life and Robotics*, pages 435–439. Citeseer.

Maja Djikic, Keith Oatley, Sara Zoeterman, and Jordan B Peterson. 2009a. Defenseless against art? impact of reading fiction on emotion in avoidantly attached individuals. *Journal of Research in Personality*, 43(1):14–17.

Maja Djikic, Keith Oatley, Sara Zoeterman, and Jordan B Peterson. 2009b. On being moved by art: How reading fiction transforms the self. *Creativity Research Journal*, 21(1):24–29.

Cynthia Dwork, Moritz Hardt, Toniann Pitassi, Omer Reingold, and Richard Zemel. 2012. Fairness through awareness. In *Proceedings of the 3rd innovations in theoretical computer science conference*, pages 214–226. ACM.

Leah East, Debra Jackson, Louise O'Brien, and Kathleen Peters. 2010. Storytelling: an approach that can help to develop resilience. *Nurse Researcher (through 2013)*, 17(3):17–25.

David K Elson. 2012. *Modeling narrative discourse*. Columbia University.

Malte Elson, Johannes Breuer, James D Ivory, and Thorsten Quandt. 2014. More than stories with buttons: Narrative, mechanics, and context as determinants of player experience in digital games. *Journal of Communication*, 64(3):521–542.

Chris Fairclough and Pádraig Cunningham. 2004. Ai structuralist storytelling in computer games. Technical report, Trinity College Dublin, Department of Computer Science.

Ethan Fast, Tina Vachovsky, and Michael S Bernstein. 2016. Shirtless and dangerous: Quantifying linguistic signals of gender bias in an online fiction writing community. In *ICWSM*, pages 112–120.

Zhenxin Fu, Xiaoye Tan, Nanyun Peng, Dongyan Zhao, and Rui Yan. 2017. Style transfer in text: Exploration and evaluation. *arXiv preprint arXiv:1711.06861*.

Shira Gabriel and Ariana F Young. 2011. Becoming a vampire without being bitten: The narrative collective-assimilation hypothesis. *Psychological Science*, 22(8):990–994.

Traci Gillig and Sheila Murphy. 2016. Fostering support for lgbtq youth? the effects of a gay adolescent media portrayal on young viewers. *International Journal of Communication*, 10:23.

Melanie C Green, Timothy C Brock, and Geoff F Kaufman. 2004. Understanding media enjoyment: The role of transportation into narrative worlds. *Communication Theory*, 14(4):311–327.

Melanie C Green, Sheryl Kass, Jana Carrey, Benjamin Herzig, Ryan Feeney, and John Sabini. 2008. Transportation across media: Repeated exposure to print and film. *Media Psychology*, 11(4):512–539.

Melanie C Green, Jeffrey J Strange, and Timothy C Brock. 2003. *Narrative impact: Social and cognitive foundations*. Taylor & Francis.

Kia Groom. 2015. A call to arms: Bite the hand that feeds you.

Matthew Guzdial, Brent Harrison, Boyang Li, and Mark Riedl. 2015. Crowdsourcing open interactive narrative. In *FDG*.

Mengqiao Han, Ou Wu, and Zhendong Niu. 2017. Unsupervised automatic text style transfer using lstm. In *National CCF Conference on Natural Language Processing and Chinese Computing*, pages 281–292. Springer.

Stacey Hand and Duane Varan. 2008. Interactive narratives: Exploring the links between empathy, interactivity and structure. In *European Conference on Interactive Television*, pages 11–19. Springer.

D Fox Harrell and Jichen Zhu. 2009. Agency play: Dimensions of agency for interactive narrative design. In *AAAI spring symposium: Intelligent narrative technologies II*, pages 44–52.

Paul L Harris. 2000. Understanding childrens worlds: The work of the imagination. *Oxfo Blackwell*.

Dorothée Hefner, Christoph Klimmt, and Peter Vorderer. 2007. Identification with the player character as determinant of video game enjoyment. In *Entertainment computing–ICEC 2007*, pages 39–48. Springer.

Fritz Heider and Marianne Simmel. 1944. An experimental study of apparent behavior. *The American journal of psychology*, 57(2):243–259.

Hal E Hershfield, Susanne Scheibe, Tamara L Sims, and Laura L Carstensen. 2013. When feeling bad can be good: Mixed emotions benefit physical health across adulthood. *Social psychological and personality science*, 4(1):54–61.

Bell Hooks et al. 2006. *Black looks: Race and representation*. Academic Internet Pub Inc.

Ting-Hao Kenneth Huang, Francis Ferraro, Nasrin Mostafazadeh, Ishan Misra, Aishwarya Agrawal, Jacob Devlin, Ross Girshick, Xiaodong He, Pushmeet Kohli, Dhruv Batra, et al. 2016. Visual storytelling. In *Proceedings of the 2016 Conference of the North American Chapter of the Association for Computational Linguistics: Human Language Technologies*, pages 1233–1239.

Keenan M Jenkins. 2014. *Choose your own adventure: Interactive narratives and attitude change*. Ph.D. thesis, The University of North Carolina at Chapel Hill.

Carl Gustav Jung. 1964. *Man and his symbols*. Laurel.

Jad Kabbara and Jackie Chi Kit Cheung. 2016. Stylistic transfer in natural language generation systems using recurrent neural networks. In *Proceedings of the Workshop on Uphill Battles in Language Processing: Scaling Early Achievements to Robust Methods*, pages 43–47.

Geoff F. Kaufman and Lisa K. Libby. 2012. Changing beliefs and behavior through experience-taking. *Journal of Personality and Social Psychology*, 103(2):1–19.

David Comer Kidd and Emanuele Castano. 2013. Reading literary fiction improves theory of mind. *Science*, 342(6156):377–380.

Edith Law, Ming Yin, Joslin Goh, Kevin Chen, Michael A. Terry, and Krzysztof Z. Gajos. 2016. Curiosity killed the cat, but makes crowdwork better. In *Proceedings of the 2016 CHI Conference on Human Factors in Computing Systems*, CHI '16, pages 4098–4110, New York, NY, USA. ACM.

Michael Lebowitz. 1987. Planning stories. In *Proceedings of the 9th annual conference of the cognitive science society*, pages 234–242.

Boyang Li, Stephen Lee-Urban, Darren Scott Appling, and Mark O Riedl. 2012. Crowdsourcing narrative intelligence. *Advances in Cognitive Systems*, 2(1).

Boyang Li, Stephen Lee-Urban, and Mark Riedl. 2013. Crowdsourcing interactive fiction games. In *FDG*, pages 431–432.

Boyang Li, Mohini Thakkar, Yijie Wang, and Mark O Riedl. 2014. Data-driven alibi story telling for social believability. *Social Believability in Games*.

Brian Magerko. 2006. Player modeling in the interactive drama architecture. *Department of Computer Science and Engineering, University of Michigan.*

Inderjeet Mani. 2012. Computational modeling of narrative. *Synthesis Lectures on Human Language Technologies*, 5(3):1–142.

Marie-Louise Mares, Mary Beth Oliver, and Joanne Cantor. 2008. Age differences in adults' emotional motivations for exposure to films. *Media Psychology*, 11(4):488–511.

Michael Mateas and Andrew Stern. 2003. Façade: An experiment in building a fully-realized interactive drama. In *Game developers conference*, volume 2, pages 4–8.

Wook-Hee Min, Eok-Soo Shim, Yeo-Jin Kim, and Yun-Gyung Cheong. 2008. Planning-integrated story graph for interactive narratives. In *Proceedings of the 2Nd ACM International Workshop on Story Representation, Mechanism and Context*, SRMC '08, pages 27–32, New York, NY, USA. ACM.

Janet Murray. 2004. From game-story to cyberdrama. *First person: New media as story, performance, and game*, 1:2–11.

Jeeyun Oh, Mun-Young Chung, and Sangyong Han. 2014. The more control, the better? *Journal of Media Psychology.*

Summer Okoye. 2016. The black commodity.

Mary Beth Oliver. 1993. Exploring the paradox of the enjoyment of sad films. *Human Communication Research*, 19(3):315–342.

M.B. Oliver. 2003. Mood management and selective exposure. In Jennings Bryan, David Roskos-Ewoldsen, and Joanne Cantor, editors, *Communication and emotion: Essays in honor of Dolf Zillmann.* Routledge.

Jessica Ouyang and Kathleen McKeown. 2015. Modeling reportable events as turning points in narrative. In *Proceedings of the 2015 Conference on Empirical Methods in Natural Language Processing*, pages 2149–2158.

Vivian Gussin Paley. 2009. *A child's work: The importance of fantasy play.* University of Chicago Press.

James W Pennebaker. 1997. Writing about emotional experiences as a therapeutic process. *Psychological science*, 8(3):162–166.

Julie Porteous and Marc Cavazza. 2009. Controlling narrative generation with planning trajectories: the role of constraints. In *Joint International Conference on Interactive Digital Storytelling*, pages 234–245. Springer.

Gerald Prince. 1974. *A grammar of stories: An introduction*, volume 13. Walter de Gruyter.

Christopher Purdy and Mark O Riedl. 2016. Reading between the lines: Using plot graphs to draw inferences from stories. In *International Conference on Interactive Digital Storytelling*, pages 197–208. Springer.

Andrew J Reagan. 2017. *Towards a science of human stories: using sentiment analysis and emotional arcs to understand the building blocks of complex social systems.* Ph.D. thesis, The University of Vermont and State Agricultural College.

Mark O Riedl and Brent Harrison. 2016. Using stories to teach human values to artificial agents. In *AAAI Workshop: AI, Ethics, and Society.*

Mark O Riedl and Robert Michael Young. 2010. Narrative planning: Balancing plot and character. *Journal of Artificial Intelligence Research*, 39:217–268.

Ute Ritterfeld and Seung-A Jin. 2006. Addressing media stigma for people experiencing mental illness using an entertainment-education strategy. *Journal of health psychology*, 11(2):247–267.

Frank Rose. 2012. *The art of immersion: How the digital generation is remaking Hollywood, Madison Avenue, and the way we tell stories.* WW Norton & Company.

Alyssa Rosenberg. 2012. From Lena Dunham to Junot Díaz: How to write people who aren't you.

Paul Rozin, Lily Guillot, Katrina Fincher, Alexander Rozin, and Eli Tsukayama. 2013. Glad to be sad, and other examples of benign masochism. *Judgment and Decision Making*, 8(4):439.

Marie-Laure Ryan and A-L Rebreyend. 2013. From narrative games to playable stories. *Nouvelle revue desthétique*, (1):37–50.

Marie-Laure Ryan et al. 2007. Toward a definition of narrative. *The Cambridge companion to narrative*, pages 22–35.

Kimiko Ryokai and Justine Cassell. 1999. Storymat: a play space for collaborative storytelling. In *CHI'99 extended abstracts on Human factors in computing systems*, pages 272–273. ACM.

Maarten Sap, Marcella Cindy Prasettio, Ari Holtzman, Hannah Rashkin, and Yejin Choi. 2017. Connotation frames of power and agency in modern films. In *Proceedings of the 2017 Conference on Empirical Methods in Natural Language Processing*, pages 2329–2334.

Roger C Schank and Robert P Abelson. 1975. Scripts, plans, and knowledge. In *IJCAI*, pages 151–157.

Roger C Schank et al. 1975. Sam–a story understander. Research report no. 43.

Scott Selisker. 2015. The Bechdel test and the social form of character networks. *New Literary History*, 46(3):505–523.

Nisi Shawl and Cynthia Ward. 2005. *Writing the Other*. Seattle, Washington: Aqueduct Press.

Tianxiao Shen, Tao Lei, Regina Barzilay, and Tommi Jaakkola. 2017. Style transfer from non-parallel text by cross-alignment. In *Advances in Neural Information Processing Systems*, pages 6833–6844.

Michael D Slater, Donna Rouner, and Marilee Long. 2006. Television dramas and support for controversial public policies: Effects and mechanisms. *Journal of Communication*, 56(2):235–252.

Zadie Smith. 2009. Speaking in tongues. *The New York review of books*, 26:1–16.

Jiyeon So and Robin Nabi. 2013. Reduction of perceived social distance as an explanation for media's influence on personal risk perceptions: A test of the risk convergence model. *Human Communication Research*, 39(3):317–338.

Brian Sutton-Smith. 1986. Children's fiction making.

Brian Sutton-Smith. 2012. *The folkstories of children*. University of Pennsylvania Press.

Ivo Swartjes and Mariët Theune. 2006. A fabula model for emergent narrative. In *International Conference on Technologies for Interactive Digital Storytelling and Entertainment*, pages 49–60. Springer.

Jawad Syed. 2016. Oscars so white: an institutional racism perspective. *Counterpunch*.

Abraham Tesser, Joanne V Wood, and Diederik A Stapel. 2005. *Building, defending, and regulating the self: A psychological perspective*. Psychology Press.

David Thue, Vadim Bulitko, Marcia Spetch, and Eric Wasylishen. 2007. Interactive storytelling: A player modelling approach. In *AIIDE*, pages 43–48.

Tyler Tsay, Katherine Frain, and Serafima Fedorova. 2015. Best & worst literary moments of 2015.

Frederik Van Broeckhoven, Joachim Vlieghe, and Olga De Troyer. 2015. Using a controlled natural language for specifying the narratives of serious games. In *International conference on interactive digital storytelling*, pages 142–153. Springer.

Rob Voigt, Nicholas P Camp, Vinodkumar Prabhakaran, William L Hamilton, Rebecca C Hetey, Camilla M Griffiths, David Jurgens, Dan Jurafsky, and Jennifer L Eberhardt. 2017. Language from police body camera footage shows racial disparities in officer respect. *Proceedings of the National Academy of Sciences*, page 201702413.

Kurt Vonnegut. 1970. The shape of stories.

R Michael Young, Mark O Riedl, Mark Branly, Arnav Jhala, RJ Martin, and CJ Saretto. 2004. An architecture for integrating plan-based behavior generation with interactive game environments. *Journal of Game Development*, 1(1):51–70.

Jieyu Zhao, Tianlu Wang, Mark Yatskar, Vicente Ordonez, and Kai-Wei Chang. 2017. Men also like shopping: Reducing gender bias amplification using corpus-level constraints. *arXiv preprint arXiv:1707.09457*.

Linguistic Features of Helpfulness
in Automated Support for Creative Writing

Melissa Roemmele and Andrew S. Gordon

Institute for Creative Technologies, University of Southern California

roemmele@ict.usc.edu, gordon@ict.usc.edu

Abstract

We examine an emerging NLP application that supports creative writing by automatically suggesting continuing sentences in a story. The application tracks users' modifications to generated sentences, which can be used to quantify their "helpfulness" in advancing the story. We explore the task of predicting helpfulness based on automatically detected linguistic features of the suggestions. We illustrate this analysis on a set of user interactions with the application using an initial selection of features relevant to story generation.

1 Introduction

At the intersection between natural language generation, computational creativity, and human-computer interaction research is the vision of tools that directly collaborate with people in authoring creative content. With recent work on automatically generating creative language (Ghazvininejad et al., 2017; Stock and Strapparava, 2005; Veale and Hao, 2007, e.g.), this vision has started to come to fruition. One such application focuses on providing automated support to human authors for story writing. In particular, Roemmele and Gordon (2015), Khalifa et al. (2017), Manjavacas et al. (2017), and Clark et al. (2018) have developed systems that automatically generate suggestions for new sentences to continue an ongoing story.

As with other interactive language generation tasks, there is no obvious approach to evaluating these systems. The number of acceptable continuations that can be generated for a given story is open-ended, so measures that strictly rely on similarity to a constrained set of gold standard sentences, e.g. BLEU score (Papineni et al., 2002), are not ideal. Moreover, the focus of evaluation in interactive applications should be on users' judgments of the quality of the interaction. While

it is straightforward to ask users to rate generated content (McIntyre and Lapata, 2009; Pérez y Pérez and Sharples, 2001; Swanson and Gordon, 2012), self-reported ratings for global dimensions of quality (e.g. "on a scale of 1-5, how coherent is this sentence in this story?") do not necessarily provide insight into the specific characteristics that influenced these judgments, which users might not even be explicitly aware of. It is more useful to examine users' judgment on an implicit level: for example, by allowing them to adapt generated sequences. This is related to rewriting tasks in other domains like grammatical error correction (Sakaguchi et al., 2016), where annotators edit sentences to improve their perceived quality. This enables the features of the modified sequence to be compared to those of the original.

In this work, we analyze a set of user interactions with the application Creative Help (Roemmele and Gordon, 2015), where users make 'help' requests to automatically suggest new sentences in a story, which they can then freely modify. We take advantage of Creative Help's functionality that tracks authors' edits to generated sentences, resulting in an alignment between each original suggestion and its modified form. Previous work on this application compared different generation models according to the similarity between suggestions and corresponding modifications, based on the idea that more helpful suggestions will receive fewer edits. Here, we focus on quantifying suggestions according to a set of linguistic features shown by existing research to be relevant to story generation. We examine whether these features can be used to predict how much authors modify the suggestions. We propose that this type of analysis is useful for identifying the aspects of generated content authors implicitly find most helpful for writing. It can inform the evaluation of future creativity support systems in terms of how

Proceedings of the First Workshop on Storytelling, pages 14–19
New Orleans, Louisiana, June 5, 2018. ©2018 Association for Computational Linguistics

well they maximize features associated with help-fulness.

2 Application

The Creative Help interface consists simply of a text box where users can write a story. Authors are instructed that they can type *help*\\ at any point while writing in order to generate a suggestion for a new sentence in the story, and that they can freely modify this suggestion like any other text that already appears in the story. As soon as the suggested sentence appears to the author, the application starts tracking any edits the author makes to it. Once one minute has elapsed since the author last edited the sentence, the application logs the modified sentence alongside its original version. See Roemmele and Gordon (2015) for further details about this tracking and logging functionality. The result of authors' interactions with the application is a dataset aligning generated suggestions to their corresponding modifications along with the story context that precedes the help request.

The current generation model integrated into Creative Help is a Recurrent Neural Network Language Model (RNN LM) with Gated Recurrent Units (GRUs) that generates sentences through iterative random sampling of its probability distribution, as described in Roemmele and Gordon (2018). The motivation for this baseline model is that by training it on a corpus of fiction stories, it produces sequences that are likely to appear in these stories, but the unpredictability associated with random sampling yields novel word combinations that may be appealing from the standpoint of creativity (Boden, 2004; Dartnall, 2013; Liapis et al., 2016). The RNN LM was trained on a subset of the BookCorpus[1] (Kiros et al., 2015), which contains freely available fiction books uploaded by authors to smashwords.com. The subset included 8032 books from a variety of genres, which were split into 155,400 chapters (a little over half a billion words). To prepare the dataset for training, the stories were tokenized into lowercased words. All punctuation was treated in the same way as words. A vocabulary of all words occurring at least 25 times in the text was established, which resulted in 64,986 unique words being included in the model. All other words were mapped to a generic <UNKNOWN> token that was restricted from being generated. Proper names were

handled uniquely by replacing them with a token indicating their entity type and a unique numerical identifier for that entity (e.g. <PERSON1>). During generation, a list of all entities mentioned prior to the help request was maintained. When the model generated one of these abstract entity tokens, it was replaced with an entity of the corresponding type and numerical index in the story. If no such entity type was found in the story, an entity was randomly sampled from a list of entities found in the training data.

The RNN[2] was set up with a 300-dimension word embedding layer and two 500-dimension GRU layers. It was trained for one single iteration through all chapters, which were observed in batches of 125. The Adam algorithm (Kingma and Ba, 2015) was used for optimization. To generate a sentence when a help request was made, the model observed all text prior to the help request (the context) to compute a probability distribution for the next word. A word was sampled from this distribution, appended to the story, and this process was repeated to generate 35 words. All words after the first detected sentence boundary[3] were then filtered (in some cases, no sentence boundary was detected so all 35 words were included in the returned sentence). Finally, the suggestion was 'detokenized' using some heuristics for punctuation formatting, capitalization, and merging contractions before being presented to the author.

3 Experiment and Analyses

We recruited people via social media, email, and Amazon Mechanical Turk to interact with Creative Help[4] for at least fifteen minutes. Participants were asked to write a story of their choice. They were told the objective of the task was to experiment with asking for \\help\\ but they were not required to make a certain number of help requests. They could choose to edit, add to, or delete a suggestion just like any other text in their story, without any requirement to change the suggestion at all. Ultimately, 139 users participated in the task, resulting in suggestion-modification pairs for 940 help requests, which includes pairs where the suggestion and modification are equivalent because no edits were made.

Given this dataset of pairs, we first quantified

---

[1] yknzhu.wixsite.com/mbweb

[2] Code at: github.com/roemmele
[3] Based on spaCy's sentence segmentation: spacy.io
[4] https://fiction.ict.usc.edu/creativehelp/

Initial Story: I knew it wasn't a good idea to put the alligator in the bathtub. The problem was that there was nowhere else waterproof in the house, and Dale was going to be home in twenty minutes.	**Suggested:** I needed to know, too, and I was glad I was feeling it. **Modified:** I needed to know how upset he would be if he found out about my adoption spree.
Initial Story: My brother was a quiet boy. He liked to spend time by himself in his room and away from others. It wasn't such a bad thing, as it allowed him to focus on his more creative side. He would write books, draw comics, and write lyrics for songs that he would learn to play as he got older.	**Suggested:** He'd have to learn to get in touch with my father. **Modified:** He had an ok relationship with my parents, but mostly because they supported his separation.

Table 1: Examples of generated suggestions and corresponding modifications with their preceding context

the degree to which authors edited the suggestions. In particular, we calculated the similarity between each suggestion and corresponding modification in terms of Levenshtein edit distance: $1 - \frac{dist(sug,mod)}{max(|sug|,|mod|)}$, where higher values indicate more similarity. The mean similarity score for this dataset was 0.695 (SD=0.346), indicating that authors most often chose to retain large parts of the suggestions instead of fully rewriting them. We investigated whether these similarity scores could be predicted by the linguistic features of the suggestions. Features that significantly correlate with Levenshtein similarity can be interpreted as being 'helpful' in influencing authors to make use of the original suggestion in their story. It is certainly possible to use other similarity metrics to quantify helpfulness, such as similarity in terms of word embeddings. These measures may model similarity below the surface text of the suggestion, in which the modification may use different words to alternatively express the same story event or idea.

With this approach, given a metric for any feature, the helpfulness of that feature can be quantified. Here, we selected some features used in previous work on story generation and evaluating writing quality. In particular, we included some features used in systems applied to the Story Cloze Test (Mostafazadeh et al., 2016), which involves selecting the most likely ending for a given story from a provided set of candidates. Roemmele et al. (2017a) also explored some of these metrics to compare different models for sentence-based story continuation in an offline framework. Our metrics consist of those that analyze the individual features of a sentence by itself (story-independent, Metrics 1-7 below), and those that analyze the sentence with reference to the story context that precedes the suggestion (story-dependent, Metrics 8-14 below). For the story-dependent metrics, we only considered suggestions that did not appear as the first sentence in the story (910 suggestions).

Sentence Length: The length of a candidate ending in the Story Cloze Test was found to predict its correctness (Bugert et al., 2017; Schwartz et al., 2017). We measured the length of suggestion in terms of its number of words (Metric 1).

Grammaticality: Grammaticality is an obvious feature of high-quality writing. We used Language Tool[5] (Miłkowski, 2010), a rule-based system that detects various grammatical errors. This system computed an overall grammaticality score for each sentence, equal to the proportion of total words in the sentence deemed to be grammatically correct (Metric 2).

Lexical Frequency: Writing quality has been found to correlate with the use of unique words (Burstein and Wolska, 2003; Crossley et al., 2011). We computed the average frequency of the words in each suggestion according to their Good-Turing smoothed counts in the Reddit Comment Corpus[6] (Metric 3).

Syntactic Complexity: Writing quality is also associated with greater syntactic complexity (McNamara et al., 2010; Pitler and Nenkova, 2008). We examined this feature in terms of the number and length of syntactic phrases in the generated sentences. Phrase length was approximated by the number of children under each head verb/noun as given by the dependency parse. We counted the total number of noun phrases (Metric 4) and words per noun phrase (Metric 5), and likewise the number of verb phrases (Metric 6) and words per verb phrase (Metric 7). These metrics were all normalized by sentence length.

Lexical Cohesion: Correct endings in the Story Cloze Test tend to have higher lexical similarity to their contexts according to statistical measures of similarity (Mihaylov and Frank, 2017; Mostafazadeh et al., 2016; Flor and Somasundaran, 2017). We analyzed lexical cohesion be-

---

[5] Code at: pypi.python.org/pypi/language-check
[6] spacy.io/docs/api/token

16

tween the context and suggestion in terms of their Jaccard similarity (proportion of overlapping words; Metric 8), GloVe word embeddings[7] trained on the Common Crawl corpus (Metric 9), and sentence (skip-thought) vectors[8] (Kiros et al., 2015) trained on the BookCorpus (Metric 10). For the latter two, the score was the cosine similarity between the means of the context and suggestion vectors, respectively.

Style Consistency: Automated measures of writing style have been used to predict the success of fiction novels (Ganjigunte Ashok et al., 2013). Moreover, Schwartz et al. (2017) found that simple n-gram style features could distinguish between correct and incorrect endings in the Story Cloze Test. We examined the similarity in style between the context and suggestion in terms of their distributions of coarse-grained part-of-speech tags, using the same approach as Ireland and Pennebaker (2010). The similarity between the context c and suggestion s for each POS category was quantified as $1 - \frac{|pos_c - pos_s|}{pos_c + pos_s}$, where pos is the proportion of words with that tag. We averaged the scores across all POS categories (Metric 11). We also looked at style in terms of the Jaccard similarity between the POS trigrams in the context and suggestion (Metric 12).

Sentiment Similarity: The relation between the sentiment of a story and a candidate ending in the Story Cloze Test can be used to predict its correctness (Flor and Somasundaran, 2017; Goel and Singh, 2017; Bugert et al., 2017). We applied sentiment analysis to the context and suggestion using the tool[9] described in Staiano and Guerini (2014), which provides a valence score for 11 emotions. For each emotion, we computed the inverse distance $\frac{1}{(1+|e_c - e_s|)}$ between the context and suggestion scores e_c and e_s, respectively. We averaged these values across all emotions to get one overall sentiment similarity score (Metric 13).

Entity Coreference: Events in stories are linked by common entities (e.g. characters, locations, and objects), so coreference between entity mentions is particularly important for establishing the coherence of a story (Elsner, 2012). We calculated the proportion of entities in each suggestion that coreferred to an entity in the corresponding context[10] (Metric 14).

---

[7]nlp.stanford.edu/projects/glove
[8]github.com/ryankiros/skip-thoughts
[9]github.com/marcoguerini/DepecheMood/releases
[10]Using CoreNLP: stanfordnlp.github.io/CoreNLP

4 Results and Conclusion

	ρ
1. Sentence length	-0.082
2. Grammaticality	0.097
3. Word frequency	0.058
4. # NPs	0.112
5. NP length	0.052
6. # VPs	0.001
7. VP length	-0.022
8. Jaccard sim	0.017
9. GloVe sim	0.105
10. Skip-thought sim	0.258
11. Word POS sim	-0.037
12. Trigram POS sim	-0.023
13. Sentiment sim	0.107
14. Coreference	0.134

Table 2: Correlation ρ between metric scores for suggestions and similarity to modifications

Table 2 shows the Spearman correlation coefficient (ρ) between the suggestion scores for each metric and their Levenshtein similarity to the resulting modifications. This coefficient indicates the degree to which the corresponding feature predicted authors' modifications, where higher coefficients mean that authors applied fewer edits. Statistically significant correlations (p < 0.005) are highlighted in gray, indicating that suggestions with higher scores on these metrics were particularly helpful to authors. Suggestion length did not have a significant impact, but grammaticality emerged as a helpful feature. The frequency scores of the words in the suggestions did not significantly influence their helpfulness. In terms of syntactic complexity, suggestions with more noun phrases were edited less often, but verb complexity was not influential. For lexical cohesion, the number of overlapping words between the suggestion and its context (Jaccard similarity) was not predictive, but vector-based similarity was an indicator of helpfulness. Similarity in terms of sentence (skip-thought) vectors was the most helpful feature overall, which suggests these representations are indeed useful for modeling coherence between neighboring sentences in a story. Analogously, Roemmele et al. (2017b) and Srinivasan et al. (2018) found that these representations were very effective for encoding story sentences in the Story Cloze Test in order to predict correct endings. Neither metric for style similarity predicted authors' edits, but sentiment similarity between the suggestion and context was significantly helpful. Finally, suggestions that more frequently coreferred to entities introduced in the context were more helpful.

These results describe this particular sample of Creative Help interactions for a selected set of features relevant to story generation, but this analysis can be scaled to determine the influence of any feature in an automated writing support framework where authors can adapt generated content. The objective of this approach is to leverage data from user interactions with the system to establish an automated feedback loop for evaluation, by which features that emerge as helpful can be promoted in future systems.

Acknowledgments

The projects or efforts depicted were or are sponsored by the U.S. Army. The content or information presented does not necessarily reflect the position or the policy of the Government, and no official endorsement should be inferred.

References

Margaret A Boden. 2004. *The creative mind: Myths and mechanisms*. Psychology Press.

Michael Bugert, Yevgeniy Puzikov, Andreas Rücklé, Judith Eckle-Kohler, Teresa Martin, Eugenio Martínez-Cámara, Daniil Sorokin, Maxime Peyrard, and Iryna Gurevych. 2017. LSDSem 2017: Exploring data generation methods for the story cloze test. In *LSDSem 2017*.

Jill Burstein and Magdalena Wolska. 2003. Toward Evaluation of Writing Style: Finding Overly Repetitive Word Use in Student Essays. In *Proceedings of the Tenth Conference on European Chapter of the Association for Computational Linguistics*. Association for Computational Linguistics, Stroudsburg, PA, USA, pages 35–42.

Elizabeth Clark, Anne Ross, Chenhao Tan, Yangfeng Ji, and Noah A. Smith. 2018. Creative Writing with a Machine in the Loop: Case Studies on Slogans and Stories. In *Proceedings of the 23rd ACM Conference on Intelligent User Interfaces*. IUI'2018.

Scott A. Crossley, Jennifer L. Weston, Susan T. McLain Sullivan, and Danielle S. McNamara. 2011. The Development of Writing Proficiency as a Function of Grade Level: A Linguistic Analysis. *Written Communication* 28(3):282–311.

Terry Dartnall. 2013. *Artificial intelligence and creativity: An interdisciplinary approach*, volume 17. Springer Science & Business Media.

Micha Elsner. 2012. Character-based Kernels for Novelistic Plot Structure. In *Proceedings of the 13th Conference of the European Chapter of the Association for Computational Linguistics*. EACL '12.

Michael Flor and Swapna Somasundaran. 2017. Sentiment Analysis and Lexical Cohesion for the Story Cloze Task. In *LSDSem 2017*.

Vikas Ganjigunte Ashok, Song Feng, and Yejin Choi. 2013. Success with Style: Using Writing Style to Predict the Success of Novels. In *Proceedings of the 2013 Conference on Empirical Methods in Natural Language Processing*. Association for Computational Linguistics, Seattle, Washington, USA, pages 1753–1764.

Marjan Ghazvininejad, Xing Shi, Jay Priyadarshi, and Kevin Knight. 2017. Hafez: an Interactive Poetry Generation System. In *Proceedings of ACL 2017, System Demonstrations*. Association for Computational Linguistics, pages 43–48.

Pranav Goel and Anil Kumar Singh. 2017. IIT (BHU): System Description for LSDSem17 Shared Task. In *LSDSem 2017*.

Molly E Ireland and James W Pennebaker. 2010. Language style matching in writing: synchrony in essays, correspondence, and poetry. *Journal of personality and social psychology* 99(3):549.

Ahmed Khalifa, Gabriella AB Barros, and Julian Togelius. 2017. DeepTingle. In *International Conference on Computational Creativity 2017*.

Diederik Kingma and Jimmy Ba. 2015. Adam: A method for stochastic optimization. In *The International Conference on Learning Representations*. San Diego.

Ryan Kiros, Yukun Zhu, Ruslan Salakhutdinov, Richard S. Zemel, Antonio Torralba, Raquel Urtasun, and Sanja Fidler. 2015. Skip-thought vectors. In *Proceedings of the 28th International Conference on Neural Information Processing Systems*. MIT Press, Cambridge, MA, USA, pages 3294–3302.

Antonios Liapis, Georgios N Yannakakis, Constantine Alexopoulos, and Phil Lopes. 2016. Can computers foster human users creativity? Theory and praxis of mixed-initiative co-creativity. *Digit. Cult. Educ. (DCE)* 8(2):136–152.

Enrique Manjavacas, Folgert Karsdorp, Ben Burtenshaw, and Mike Kestemont. 2017. Synthetic Literature: Writing Science Fiction in a Co-Creative Process. In *Proceedings of the Workshop on Computational Creativity in Natural Language Generation (CC-NLG 2017)*. pages 29–37.

Neil McIntyre and Mirella Lapata. 2009. Learning to Tell Tales: A Data-driven Approach to Story Generation. In *Proceedings of the Joint Conference of the 47th Annual Meeting of the ACL and the 4th International Joint Conference on Natural Language Processing of the AFNLP*. Association for Computational Linguistics, Stroudsburg, PA, USA, pages 217–225.

Danielle S. McNamara, Scott A. Crossley, and Philip M. McCarthy. 2010. Linguistic features of writing quality. *Written Communication* 27(1):57–86.

Todor Mihaylov and Anette Frank. 2017. Story Cloze ending selection baselines and data examination. In *LSDSem 2017*.

Marcin Miłkowski. 2010. Developing an open-source, rule-based proofreading tool. *Softw. Pract. Exper.* 40(7):543–566.

Nasrin Mostafazadeh, Nathanael Chambers, Xiaodong He, Devi Parikh, Dhruv Batra, Lucy Vanderwende, Pushmeet Kohli, and James Allen. 2016. A Corpus and Cloze Evaluation for Deeper Understanding of Commonsense Stories. In *Proceedings of the 14th Annual Conference of the North American Chapter of the Association for Computational Linguistics: Human Language Technologies (NAACL HLT 2016)*. pages 839–849.

Kishore Papineni, Salim Roukos, Todd Ward, and Wei-Jing Zhu. 2002. BLEU: a method for automatic evaluation of machine translation. In *Proceedings of the 40th Annual Meeting on Association for Computational Linguistics*. Association for Computational Linguistics, pages 311–318.

Rafael Pérez y Pérez and Mike Sharples. 2001. MEXICA: A computer model of a cognitive account of creative writing. *Journal of Experimental & Theoretical Artificial Intelligence* 13(2):119–139.

Emily Pitler and Ani Nenkova. 2008. Revisiting readability: A unified framework for predicting text quality. In *Proceedings of the Conference on Empirical Methods in Natural Language Processing*. Association for Computational Linguistics, Stroudsburg, PA, USA, pages 186–195.

Melissa Roemmele and Andrew S Gordon. 2015. Creative Help: A Story Writing Assistant. In *International Conference on Interactive Digital Storytelling*. Springer International Publishing.

Melissa Roemmele and Andrew S. Gordon. 2018. Automated Assistance for Creative Writing with an RNN Language Model. In *Proceedings of the 23rd International Conference on Intelligent User Interfaces Companion*. ACM, New York, NY, USA, IUI'18, pages 21:1–21:2.

Melissa Roemmele, Andrew S Gordon, and Reid Swanson. 2017a. Evaluating Story Generation Systems Using Automated Linguistic Analyses. In *SIGKDD 2017 Workshop on Machine Learning for Creativity*.

Melissa Roemmele, Sosuke Kobayashi, Naoya Inoue, and Andrew Gordon. 2017b. An RNN-based Binary Classifier for the Story Cloze Test. In *LSDSem 2017*.

Keisuke Sakaguchi, Courtney Napoles, Matt Post, and Joel Tetreault. 2016. Reassessing the Goals of Grammatical Error Correction: Fluency Instead of Grammaticality. *Transactions of the Association for Computational Linguistics* 4:169–182.

Roy Schwartz, Maarten Sap, Ioannis Konstas, Leila Zilles, Yejin Choi, and Noah A Smith. 2017. The Effect of Different Writing Tasks on Linguistic Style: A Case Study of the ROC Story Cloze Task. In *The SIGNLL Conference on Computational Natural Language Learning (CoNLL 2017)*.

Siddarth Srinivasan, Richa Arora, and Mark Riedl. 2018. A Simple and Effective Approach to the Story Cloze Test. In *Proceedings of the 16th Annual Conference of the North American Chapter of the Association for Computational Linguistics: Human Language Technologies (NAACL HLT 2018)*.

Jacopo Staiano and Marco Guerini. 2014. DepecheMood: A lexicon for emotion analysis from crowd-annotated news. In *Proceedings of the 52nd Annual Meeting of the Association for Computational Linguistics (Short Papers)*.

Oliviero Stock and Carlo Strapparava. 2005. The act of creating humorous acronyms. *Applied Artificial Intelligence* 19(2):137–151.

Reid Swanson and Andrew S. Gordon. 2012. Say Anything: Using Textual Case-Based Reasoning to Enable Open-Domain Interactive Storytelling. *ACM Transactions on Interactive Intelligent Systems* 2(3):1–35.

Tony Veale and Yanfen Hao. 2007. Comprehending and generating apt metaphors: a web-driven, case-based approach to figurative language. In *Proceedings of AAAI*.

A Pipeline for Creative Visual Storytelling

Stephanie M. Lukin, Reginald Hobbs, Clare R. Voss
U.S. Army Research Laboratory
Adelphi, MD, USA
stephanie.m.lukin.civ@mail.mil

Abstract

Computational visual storytelling produces a textual description of events and interpretations depicted in a sequence of images. These texts are made possible by advances and cross-disciplinary approaches in natural language processing, generation, and computer vision. We define a computational creative visual storytelling as one with the ability to alter the telling of a story along three aspects: to speak about different environments, to produce variations based on narrative goals, and to adapt the narrative to the audience. These aspects of creative storytelling and their effect on the narrative have yet to be explored in visual storytelling. This paper presents a pipeline of task-modules, Object Identification, Single-Image Inferencing, and Multi-Image Narration, that serve as a preliminary design for building a creative visual storyteller. We have piloted this design for a sequence of images in an annotation task. We present and analyze the collected corpus and describe plans towards automation.

1 Introduction

Telling stories from multiple images is a creative challenge that involves visually analyzing the images, drawing connections between them, and producing language to convey the message of the narrative. To computationally model this creative phenomena, a visual storyteller must take into consideration several aspects that will influence the narrative: the environment and presentation of imagery (Madden, 2006), the narrative goals which affect the desired response of the reader or listener (Bohanek et al., 2006; Thorne and McLean, 2003), and the audience, who may prefer to read or hear different narrative styles (Thorne, 1987).

The environment is the content of the imagery, but also its interpretability (e.g., image quality). Canonical images are available from a number of high-quality datasets (Everingham et al., 2010; Plummer et al., 2015; Lin et al., 2014; Ordonez et al., 2011), however, there is little coverage of low-resourced domains with low-quality images or atypical camera perspectives that might appear in a sequence of pictures taken from blind persons, a child learning to use a camera, or a robot surveying a site. For this work, we studied an environment with odd surroundings taken from a camera mounted on a ground robot.

Narrative goals guide the selection of what objects or inferences in the image are relevant or uncharacteristic. The result is a narrative tailored to different goals such as a general "describe the scene", or a more focused "look for suspicious activity". The most salient narrative may shift as new information, in the form of images, is presented, offering different possible interpretations of the scene. This work posed a forensic task with the narrative goal to describe what may have occurred within a scene, assuming some temporal consistency across images. This open-endedness evoked creativity in the resulting narratives.

The telling of the narrative will also differ based upon the target audience. A concise narrative is more appropriate if the audience is expecting to hear news or information, while a verbose and humorous narrative is suited for entertainment. Audiences may differ in how they would best experience the narrative: immersed in the first person or through an omniscient narrator. The audience in this work was unspecified, thus the audience was the same as the storyteller defining the narrative.

To build a computational creative visual storyteller that customizes a narrative along these three aspects, we propose a creative visual storytelling pipeline requiring separate task-modules for Object Identification, Single-Image Inferencing, and Multi-Image Narration. We have conducted an exploratory pilot experiment following this pipeline

Proceedings of the First Workshop on Storytelling, pages 20–32
New Orleans, Louisiana, June 5, 2018. ©2018 Association for Computational Linguistics

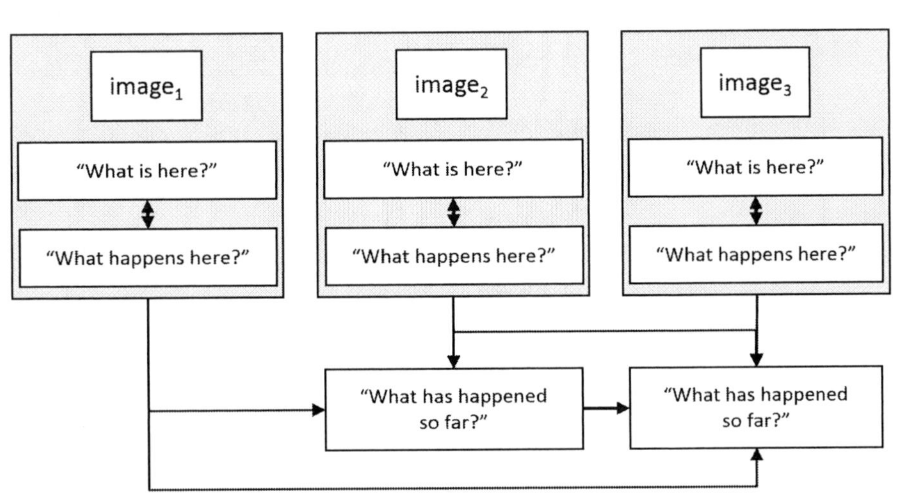

Figure 1: Creative Visual Storytelling Pipeline: T1 (Object Identification), T2 (Single Image Inferencing), T3 (Multi-Image Narration)

to collect data from each task-module to train the computational storyteller. The collected data provides instances of creative storytelling from which we have analyzed what people see and pay attention to, what they interpret, and how they weave together a story across a series of images.

Creative visual storytelling requires an understanding of the creative processes. We argue that existing systems cannot achieve these creative aspects of visual storytelling. Current object identification algorithms may perform poorly on low-resourced environments with minimal training data. Computer vision algorithms may over-identify objects, that is, describe more objects than are ultimately needed for the goal of a coherent narrative. Algorithms that generate captions of an image often produce generic language, rather than language tailored to a specific audience. Our pilot experiment is an attempt to reveal the creative processes involved when humans perform this task, and then to computationally model the phenomena from the observed data.

Our pipeline is introduced in Section 2, where we also discuss computational considerations and the application of this pipeline to our pilot experiment. In Section 3 we describe the exploratory pilot experiment, in which we presented images of a low-quality and atypical environment and have annotators answer "what may have happened here?" This open-ended narrative goal has the potential to elicit diverse and creative narratives. We did not specify the audience, leaving the annotator free to write in a style that appeals to them. The data and analysis of the pilot are presented in Section 4, as well as observations for extending to crowdsourcing a larger corpus and how to use these creative insights to build computational models that follow this pipeline. In Section 5 we compare our approach to recent works in other storytelling methodologies, then conclude and describe future directions of this work in Section 6.

2 Creative Visual Storytelling Pipeline

The pipeline and interaction of task-modules we have designed to perform creative visual storytelling over multiple images are depicted in Figure 1. Each task-module answers a question critical to creative visual storytelling: "what is here?" (T1: Object Identification), "what happens here?" (T2: Single-Image Inferencing), and "what has happened so far?" (T3: Multi-Image Narration). We discuss the purpose, expected inputs and outputs of each module, and explore computational implementations of the pipeline.

2.1 Pipeline

This section describes the task-modules we designed that provide answers to our questions for creative visual storytelling.

Task-Module 1: Object Identification (T1). Objects in an image are the building blocks for storytelling that answer the question, literally, "what is here?" This question is asked of every image in a sequence for the purposes of object curation. From a single image, the expected outputs are objects and their descriptors. We anticipate that two categories of object descriptors will be informative for interfacing with the subsequent task-modules: spatial descriptors, consisting of object *co-locations* and *orientation*, and observational *attribute* descriptors, including color, shape, or texture of the object. Confidence level will provide information about the *expectedness* of the object and its descriptors, or if the object is difficult or *uncertain* to decipher given the environment.

Task-Module 2: Single-Image Inferencing (T2). Dependent upon T1, the Single-Image Inferencing task-module is a literal interpretation derived from the objects previously identified in the context of the current image. After the curation of objects in T1, a second round of content selection commences in the form of inference determination and selection. Using the selected objects, descriptors, and expectations about the objects, this task-module answers the question "what happens here?" For example, the function of "kitchen" might be extrapolated from the co-location of a cereal box, pan, and crockpot.

Separating T2 from T1 creates a modular system where each task-module can make the best decision given the information available. However, these task-modules are also interdependent: as the inferences in T2 depend upon T1 for object selection, so too does the object selection depend upon the inferences drawn so far.

Task-Module 3: Multi-Image Narration (T3). A narrative can indeed be constructed from a single image, however, we designed our pipeline to consider when additional context, in the form of additional images, is provided. The Multi-Image Narration task-module draws from T1 and T2 to construct the larger narrative. All images, objects, and inferences are taken into consideration when determining "what has happened so far?" and "what has happened from one image to the next?" This task-module performs narrative planning by referencing the inferences and objects from the previous images. It then produces a natural language output in the form of a narrative text. Plausible narrative interpretations are formed from global knowledge about how the addition of new images confirm or disprove prior hypotheses and expectations.

2.2 From Pipeline Design to Pilot

Our first step towards building this automated pipeline is to pilot it. We will use the dataset collected and the results from the exploratory study to to build an informed computational, creative visual storyteller. When piloting, we refer to this pipeline a sequence of annotation tasks.

T1 is based on computer vision technology. Of particular interest are our collected annotations on the low-quality and atypical environments that traditionally do not have readily available object annotations. Commonsense reasoning and knowledge bases drive the technology behind deriving T2 inferences. T3 narratives consist of two sub-task-modules: narrative planning and natural language generation. Each technology can be matched to our pipeline, and be built up separately, leveraging existing works, but tuned to this task.

Our annotators are required to write in natural language (though we do not specify full sentences) the answers to the questions posed in each task-module. While this natural language intermediate representation of T1 and T2 is appropriate for a pilot study, a semantic representation of these task-modules might be more feasible for computation until the final rendering of the narrative text. For example, drawing inferences in T2 with the objects identified in T1 might be better achieved with an ontological representation of objects and attributes, such as WordNet (Fellbaum, 1998), and inferences mined from a knowledge base.

In our annotation, the sub-task-modules of narrative planning and natural language generation are implicitly intertwined. The annotator does not note in the exercise intermediary narrative planning before writing the final text. In computation, T3 may generate the final narrative text word-by-word (combining narrative planning and natural language generation). Another approach might first perform narrative planning, followed by generation from a semantic or syntactic representation that is compatible with intermediate representations from T1 and T2.

3 Pilot Experiment

A paper-based pilot experiment implementing this pipeline was conducted. Ten annotators (A_1 - A_{10})[1] participated in the annotation of the three

---

[1] A_5, an author of this paper, designed the experiment and examples. All annotators had varying degrees of familiarity with the environment in the images.

Figure 2: image$_1$, image$_2$, and image$_3$ in Pilot Experiment Scene

images in Figure 2 (image$_1$ - image$_3$). These images were taken from a camera mounted on a ground robot while it navigated an unfamiliar environment. The environment was static, thus, presenting these images in temporal order was not as critical as it would have been if the images were still-frames taken from a video or if the images contained a progression of actions or events.

Annotators first addressed the questions posed in the Object Identification (T1) and Single-Image Inference (T2) task-modules for image$_1$. They repeated the process for image$_2$ and image$_3$, and authored a Multi-Image Narrative (T3). The annotator work flow mimicked the pipeline presented in Figure 1. For each subsequent image, the time allotted increased from five, to eight, to eleven minutes to allow more time for the narrative to be constructed after annotators processed the additional images. An example image sequence with answers was provided prior to the experiment. A$_5$ gave a brief, oral, open-ended explanation of the experiment as not to bias annotators to what they should focus on in the scene or what kind of language they should use. The goal of this data collection is to gather data that models the creative storytelling processes, not to track these processes in real-time. A future web-based interface will allow us to track the timing of annotation, what information is added when, and how each task-module influences the other task-modules for each image.

Object Identification did not require annotators to define a bounding box for labeled objects, nor were annotators required to provide objective descriptors[2]. Annotators authored natural language labels, phrases, or sentences to describe objects, attributes, and spatial relations while indicating

confidence levels if appropriate.

During Single Image Inferencing, annotators were shown their response from T1 as they authored a natural language description of activity or functions of the image, as well as a natural language explanation of inferences for that determination, citing supporting evidence from T1 output. For a single image, annotators may answer the questions posed by T1 and T2 in any order to build the most informed narrative.

Annotators authored a Multi-Image Narrative to explain what has happened in the sequence of images presented so far. For each image seen in the sequence, annotators were shown their own natural language responses from T1 and T2 for those images. Annotators were encouraged to look back to their responses in previous images (as the bottom row of Figure 1 indicates), but not to make changes to their responses about the previous images. They were, however, encouraged to incorporate previous feedback into the context of the current image. From this task-module, annotators wrote a natural language narrative connecting activity or functions in the images which will be used to learn how to weave together a story across the images.

The open-ended "what has happened here?" narrative goal has no single answer. These annotations may be treated as ground truth, but we run the risk of potentially missing out on creative alternatives. Bootstraping all possible objects and inferences would achieve greater coverage, yet this quickly becomes infeasible. We lean toward the middle, where the answers collected will help determine what annotators deem as important.

4 Results and Analysis

In this section, we discuss and analyze the collected data and provide insights for incorporating each task-module into a computational system.

---

[2]As we design a web-based version of this experiment, we will enforce interfaces explicitly linked to object annotations, and the desire to view previously annotated images.

# Annotators	Objects
10	calendar, water bottle
9	computer, table/desk
8	chair
4	walls, window
2	blue triangles
1	floor, praying rug

Table 1: Objects identified by annotators in $image_1$

# Annotators	Objects
10	suitcase, shirt
8	sign
6	green object
5	fire extinguisher
4	walls
3	bag
2	floor, window
1	coat hanger, shoes, rug

Table 2: Objects identified by annotators in $image_2$

# Annotators	Objects
7	crockpot, cereal box, table
6	pan
5	container
2	walls, label
1	thread and needle, coffee pot, jam, door frame

Table 3: Objects identified by annotators in $image_3$ (total of 7 annotators)

4.1 Object Identification (T1)

Thirty three objects were identified across the images.[3] A_5 identified the most of these objects (20), and A_1, the least (10). Tables 1 - 3 show the objects identified and how many annotators referenced each object. A set of objects emerged in each image that captured the annotators' attention. Object descriptor categories are tabulated in Table 4[4]. Not surprisingly, the most common descriptors were attributes, e.g., color and shape, followed by co-locations. Orientation was not observed in this dataset, however this category may be useful for other disrupted environments. We observed instances of uncertainty, e.g., "a suitcase, not entirely sure, because of zipper and size", and unexpected objects, "unfinished floor", whereas "floors" may have not been labeled otherwise.

Lack of coverage and overlap in this task with respect to objects and descriptors is not discouraging. In fact, we argue that exhaustive object

	Total	Average	Min	Max
Spatial				
Co-Location	51	6.3	0	14
Observational				
Attribute	99	12.2	3	22
Confidence				
Unexpected	7	0.7	0	4
Uncertainty	28	3.3	0	8
Total	185	22.6	7	39

Table 4: Object descriptor summary with counts per annotator (A_2 - A_4 excluded from average, min, and max; see footnote 4)

identification is counter-intuitive and detrimental to creative visual storytelling. Annotators may have identified only the objects of interest to the narrative they were forming, and viewed other objects as distractors. The most frequent of the identified objects are likely to be the most influential in T2 where the calendar, computer, and chair provide more information than the "blue triangles".

Not only can selective object identification provide the most salient objects for deriving interpretations, but the Object Identification exercise with respect to storytelling can differentiate between objects and descriptors that are commonplace or otherwise irrelevant. For instance, if a fire extinguisher was not annotated as red, we are inclined to deduce it is because this fact is well known or unimportant, rather than the result of a distracted annotator.[5]

When automating this task-module, new object identification algorithms should account for the following: a sampling of relevant objects specific to the storytelling challenge, and attention to potential outlier descriptors which may be more indicative than a standard descriptor, depending on the environment.

4.2 Single-Images Inferencing (T2)

We highlight A_1 and A_8 for the remainder of the discussion[6]. Table 5 shows A_1's annotation of Single-Image Inferencing and Multi-Image Narration. In the Single-Image Inferencing (T2) for $image_1$, A_1 noted the "office" theme by referencing the desk and computer, and expressed uncertainty with respect to the window looking "weird" and unlike a typical office building. A_1 kept clear

---

[3]Due to time constrains, A_2 - A_4 did not complete $image_3$.

[4]Tabulation of descriptors in Tables 7 - 9 in Appendix.

[5]We expect this to be revealed in the web-based version of the task with a stricter annotation interface.

[6]Other annotation results in Tables 10 - 17 in Appendix.

Image	Single-Image Inference	Multi-Image Narrative
Image$_1$	Looks like a dingy, sparse office. The *computer desk, calendar* indicate an office, but the space is unfinished (*no dry wall, carpet*) and area outside *window* looks weird, not like an office building.	
Image$_2$	Looks like someone was staying here temporarily, using this now to store *clothes*, or maybe as a bedroom. Again, it's atypical because its an *unfinished space* that looks uncomfortable.	I think this person was hiding out here to get ready for some event. The space isn't finished enough to be intended for habitation, but someone had to stay here, perhaps because they didn't want to be found, and you wouldn't expect someone to be living in a construction zone.
Image$_3$	This area was used as a sort of kitchen or *food storage* prep area.	Someone was definitely living here even though it wasn't finished or intended to be a house. They were probably using a crock pot because you can make food in this without having larger appliances like a stove, oven. There's no milk, so this person may be lactose intolerant. The robot should vanquish them with milk.

Table 5: A$_1$'s annotation (previously identified objects in Single-Image Inference text in italics)

Image	Single-Image Inference	Multi-Image Narrative
Image$_1$	This is likely a workplace of some sort. It is unclear if it is an *unfinished part* of a current/suspended construction project or it is just a utilitarian space inside of an industrial facility. The presence of a *computer monitor* suggest it is in use or a low crime area.	
Image$_2$	This is a jobsite of some sort. It has *unfinished walls* and what may be a *paper shredder*.	This is an unfinished building. There is some evidence of office-type work (i.e. work involving paper and computers). The existence of "windows" between rooms suggests that this is not a dwelling (or intended to become one), that is, a building designed to be a dwelling, but what it is remains unclear.
Image$_3$	A room in a building is being used as a cooking and eating station, based upon presence of *food, table,* and *cooking instruments*.	This building is being used by a likely small number of individuals for unclear purposes including cooking, eating, and basic office work.

Table 6: A$_8$'s annotation (previously identified objects in Single-Image Inference text in italics)

the distinction between images in their annotation of image$_2$, as there were no references to the office observed only in image$_1$. Instead, references in image$_2$ were to the storage of clothes. In the single-image interpretation of image$_3$, A$_1$ suggested that this was a food preparation area from the presence of the crockpot, cereal, and the other food items that appeared together. A$_8$, whose annotation is in Table 6, also noted the "workplace" theme from the desk and computer, though A$_8$ leaned more towards a construction site, citing the utilitarian space. Due to uncertainty of the environment, A$_8$ misidentified the suitcase in image$_2$ as a shredder, and incorporated it prominently into their interpretation. Similar to A$_1$, A$_8$ also indicated in image$_3$ that this was a food preparation area.

A$_8$'s misinterpretation of the suitcase raises an implementation question: are the inferences and algorithms we develop only as good as our environment data allows them to be? How might a misunderstanding of the environment affect the inferences? This environment showcased the uniqueness of the physical space and low-quality of images, yet all annotators indicated, without prompting or instruction, varying degrees of confidence in their interpretations based upon the evidence. A$_8$ indicated their uncertainty about the suitcase object by hedging that it was "what may be a paper shredder". This expression of uncertainty should be preserved in an automated system for instances such as this when an answer is unknown or has a low confidence level.

T2 is intended to inform a commonsense reasoner and knowledge base based on T1 to deduce the setting. This task-module describes functions of rooms or spaces, e.g., food preparation areas and office space. Additional interpretations about the space were made by annotators from the overall appearance of objects in the image, such as the atmospheric observation "lighting of rooms is not very good" (A_7, Table 15 in Appendix). These inferences might not be easily deducible from T1 alone, but the combination of these task-modules allows for these to occur.

Evaluating this annotation in a computational system will require some ground truth, though we have previously stated that it is impossible to claim such a gold standard in a creative storytelling task. Evaluation must therefore be subject to both qualitative and quantitative analyses, including, but not limited to, commonsense reasoning on validation sets and determining plausible alternatives to commonsense interpretations.

4.3 Multi-Image Narration (T3)

The narrative begins to form across the first two images in the Multi-Image Narration task-module (T3). A_1 hypothesized that someone was "hiding out", going a step beyond their T2 inference of an "office space" in $image_1$, to extrapolate "what has happened here" rather than "what happens here". In $image_2$, A_1 had hedged their narrative with "I think", but the language became stronger and more confident in $image_3$, in which A_1 "definitely" thought that the space was inhabited. A_1 pointed out that a lack of milk was unexpected in a canonical kitchen, and supplemented their narrative with a joke, suggesting to "vanquish them with milk". In $image_2$, A_8 interpreted that the space was not intended for long-term dwelling. Their narrative shifted in $image_3$ when another scene was revealed. A_8 concluded that this space was inhabited by a group, despite the annotator's previous assumption in $image_2$ that it was not suited for this purpose.

There is no a guaranteed "correct" narrative that unfolds, especially if we are seeking creativity. Some narrative pieces may fall into place as additional images provided context, but in the case of these environments, annotators were challenged to make sense of the sequence and pull together a plausible, if not uncertain, narrative.

The narrative goal and audience aspects of creative visual storytelling will directly inform T3. A variety of creative narratives and interpretations emerged from this pilot, despite the particularly sparse and odd environment and openness of the narrative goal. Based on the responses from each successive task-modules, all annotators' interpretations and narratives are correct. Even with anno-

tator misunderstandings, the narratives presented were their own interpretation of the environment. As the audience in this task was not specified, annotators could use any style to tell their story. The data collected expressed creativity through jokes (A_1), lists and structured information (A_5), concise deductions (A_6, A_8), uncertain deductions (A_4), first person (A_1, A_3, A_5), omniscient narrators (A_2), and the use of "we" inclusive of the robot navigating the space (A_7, A_9, A_{10}).

Future annotations may assign an audience or a style prompt in order to observe the varied language use. This will inform computational models by curating stylistic features and learning from appropriate data sources.

5 Related work

Visual storytelling is still a relatively new subfield of research that has not yet begun to capture the highly creative stories generated by text-based storytelling systems to date. The latter supports the definition of specific goals or presents alternate narrative interpretations by generating stories according to character goals (e.g., Meehan (1977)) and author goals (e.g., Lebowitz (1985)). Other interactive, co-constructed, text-based narrative systems make use of information retrieval methods by implicitly linking the text generation to the interpretation. As a result, systems incorporating these methods cannot be adjusted for different narrative goals or audiences (Cychosz et al., 2017; Swanson and Gordon, 2008; Munishkina et al., 2013).

Other research in text-based storytelling focuses on answering the question "what happens next?" to infer the selection of the most appropriate next sentence. This method indirectly relies on the selection of sentences to evaluation the results of a forced choice between the "best" or "correct" next sentence of the choices when given a narrative context (as in the Story Close Test (Mostafazadeh et al., 2016) and the Children's Book Test (Hill et al., 2015)). Our pipeline, by contrast, builds on a series of open-ended questions, for which there is no single gold-standard or reference answer. Instead, we expect in time to follow prior work by Roemmele et al. (2011) where evaluation will entail generating and ranking plausible interpretations.

Recent work on caption generation combines computer vision with a simplified narration, or single sentence text description of an image (Vinyals et al., 2015). Image processing typically takes place in one phase, while text generation follows in a second phase. Superficially, this separation of phases resembles the division of labor in our approach, where T1 and T2 involve image-specific analysis, and T3 involves text generation. However this form of caption generation depends solely on training data where individual images are paired with individual sentences. It assumes the T3 sub-task-modules can be learned from the same data source, and generates the same sentences on a per-image basis, regardless of the order of images. One can readily imagine the inadequacy of stringing together captions to construct a narrative, where the same captions describe both images of a waterfall flowing down, and those same images in reverse order where instead the water seems to be flowing up.

The work most similar in approach to our visual storyteller annotation pipeline is Huang et al. (2016) who separate their tasks into three tiers: the first over single images, generating literal descriptions of images in isolation (DII), the second over multiple images, generating literal descriptions of images in sequence (DIS), and the third over multiple images, generating stories for images in sequence (SIS). While these tiers may seem analogous to ours, there are different assumptions underlying the tasks in data collection. For each task, their images are annotated independently by different annotators, while in our approach, all images are annotated by annotators performing all of our tasks. The DII task is an exhaustive object identification task on single images, yet we leave T1 up to our annotators to determine how many objects and attributes to describe in an image to avoid the potential for object over-identification. The SIS task involves a set of images over which annotators select and possibly reorder, then write one sentence per image to create a narrative, with the opportunity to skip images. In our pipeline, we have intentionally designed our task-modules to allow for the possibility of one task-module to build off of and influence one another. It is possible in our approach for an annotator's inference in T2 of one image to feed forward and affect their T1 annotations in the subsequent image, which might in turn affect the resulting T3 narrative. In short, Huang et al. (2016) capture the thread of storytelling in one tier only, their SIS condition, while our annotators build their narratives across task-modules as they progress from image to image.

6 Conclusion and Future Work

This paper introduces a creative visual storytelling pipeline for a sequence of images that delegates separate task-modules for Object Identification, Single-Image Inferencing, and Multi-Image Narration. These task-modules can be implemented to computationally describe diverse environments and customize the telling based on narrative goals and different audiences. The pilot annotation has collected data for this visual storyteller in a low-resourced environment, and analyzed how creative visual storytelling is performed in this pipeline for the purposes of training a computational, creative visual storyteller. The pipeline is grounded in narrative decision-making processes, and we expect it to perform well on both low- and high-quality datasets. Using only curated datasets, however, runs the risk of training algorithms that are not general use.

We are now positioned to conduct a crowdsourcing annotation effort, followed by an implementation of this storyteller following the outlined task-modules for automation. Our pipeline and implementation detail are algorithmically agnostic. We anticipate off-the-shelf and state-of-the-art computer vision and language generation methodologies will provide a number of baselines for creative visual storytelling: to test environments, compare an object identification algorithm trained on high-quality data against one trained on low-quality data; to test narrative goals, compare a computer vision algorithm that may over-identify objects against one focused on a specific set to form a story; to test audience, compare a caption generation algorithm that may generate generic language against one tailored to the audience desires.

The streamlined approach of our experimental annotation pipeline allows us to easily prompt for different narrative goals and audiences in future crowdsourcing to obtain and compare different narratives. Evaluation of the final narrative must take into consideration the narrative goal and audience. In addition, evaluation must balance the correctness of the interpretation with expressing creativity, as well as the grammaticality of the generated story, suggesting new quantitative and qualitative metrics must be developed.

References

Jennifer G Bohanek, Kelly A Marin, Robyn Fivush, and Marshall P Duke. 2006. Family narrative interaction and children's sense of self. *Family process*, 45(1):39–54.

Margaret Cychosz, Andrew S Gordon, Obiageli Odimegwu, Olivia Connolly, Jenna Bellassai, and Melissa Roemmele. 2017. Effective scenario designs for free-text interactive fiction. In *International Conference on Interactive Digital Storytelling*, pages 12–23. Springer.

Mark Everingham, Luc Van Gool, Christopher KI Williams, John Winn, and Andrew Zisserman. 2010. The pascal visual object classes (voc) challenge. *International journal of computer vision*, 88(2):303–338.

Christiane Fellbaum. 1998. *WordNet*. Wiley Online Library.

Felix Hill, Antoine Bordes, Sumit Chopra, and Jason Weston. 2015. The goldilocks principle: Reading children's books with explicit memory representations. *arXiv preprint arXiv:1511.02301*.

Ting-Hao Kenneth Huang, Francis Ferraro, Nasrin Mostafazadeh, Ishan Misra, Aishwarya Agrawal, Jacob Devlin, Ross Girshick, Xiaodong He, Pushmeet Kohli, Dhruv Batra, et al. 2016. Visual storytelling. In *Proceedings of the 2016 Conference of the North American Chapter of the Association for Computational Linguistics: Human Language Technologies*, pages 1233–1239.

Michael Lebowitz. 1985. Story-telling as planning and learning. *Poetics*, 14(6):483–502.

Tsung-Yi Lin, Michael Maire, Serge Belongie, James Hays, Pietro Perona, Deva Ramanan, Piotr Dollár, and C Lawrence Zitnick. 2014. Microsoft coco: Common objects in context. In *European conference on computer vision*, pages 740–755. Springer.

Matt Madden. 2006. *99 ways to tell a story: exercises in style*. Random House.

James R Meehan. 1977. Tale-spin, an interactive program that writes stories. In *Ijcai*, volume 77, pages 91–98.

Nasrin Mostafazadeh, Nathanael Chambers, Xiaodong He, Devi Parikh, Dhruv Batra, Lucy Vanderwende, Pushmeet Kohli, and James Allen. 2016. A corpus and cloze evaluation for deeper understanding of commonsense stories. In *Proceedings of NAACL-HLT*, pages 839–849.

Larissa Munishkina, Jennifer Parrish, and Marilyn A Walker. 2013. Fully-automatic interactive story design from film scripts. In *International Conference on Interactive Digital Storytelling*, pages 229–232. Springer.

Vicente Ordonez, Girish Kulkarni, and Tamara L. Berg. 2011. Im2text: Describing images using 1 million captioned photographs. In *Neural Information Processing Systems (NIPS)*.

Bryan A Plummer, Liwei Wang, Chris M Cervantes, Juan C Caicedo, Julia Hockenmaier, and Svetlana Lazebnik. 2015. Flickr30k entities: Collecting region-to-phrase correspondences for richer image-to-sentence models. In *Computer Vision (ICCV), 2015 IEEE International Conference on*, pages 2641–2649. IEEE.

Melissa Roemmele, Cosmin Adrian Bejan, and Andrew S Gordon. 2011. Choice of plausible alternatives: An evaluation of commonsense causal reasoning. In *AAAI Spring Symposium: Logical Formalizations of Commonsense Reasoning*, pages 90–95.

Reid Swanson and Andrew S Gordon. 2008. Say anything: A massively collaborative open domain story writing companion. In *Joint International Conference on Interactive Digital Storytelling*, pages 32–40. Springer.

Avril Thorne. 1987. The press of personality: A study of conversations between introverts and extraverts. *Journal of Personality and Social Psychology*, 53(4):718.

Avril Thorne and Kate C McLean. 2003. Telling traumatic events in adolescence: A study of master narrative positioning. *Connecting culture and memory: The development of an autobiographical self*, pages 169–185.

Oriol Vinyals, Alexander Toshev, Samy Bengio, and Dumitru Erhan. 2015. Show and tell: A neural image caption generator. In *Computer Vision and Pattern Recognition (CVPR), 2015 IEEE Conference on*, pages 3156–3164. IEEE.

Appendix: Additional Annotations

Object	#	Descriptor Text	#	Descriptor
Calendar	10	hanging off the table, taped to table top	4	co-location
		marked up, ink, red circle on calendar, marked with pen	4	attribute
		foreign language	1	attribute
		paper	1	attribute
		picture on top	1	attribute
Water bottle	10	on the floor, on ground, on floor	3	co-location
		to the right of table	1	co-location
		mostly empty, unclear if it has been opened	2	attribute
		plastic	2	attribute
		closed with lid	1	attribute
Computer	9	screen, black turned off; monitor, black	3	attribute
Table / Desk	9	has computer on it, [computer] on table	2	co-location
		gray, black	2	attribute
		wood	2	attribute
		metal	1	attribute
		(presumed) rectangular	1	uncertainty
Chair	8	folding	6	attribute
		metal	5	attribute
		grey	3	attribute
Walls	4	wood	1	attribute
		unfinished and showing beams, unfinished construction	3	unexpected
Window	4	in wall behind chair	1	co-location
		window to another room; perhaps chairs in other room	1	uncertainty
		no glass	1	unexpected
Blue triangles	2	blue objects in windowsill	1	unexpected
Floor	1	unfinished	1	unexpected
Praying rug	1			

Table 7: Object Identification for image$_1$

Object	#	Descriptor Text	#	Descriptor
Suitcase	10	black, orange stripes; black and red; black with red trim; blue and copper	5	attribute
		(not entirely sure) because of zipper item and size	1	uncertainty
		resembles a paper shredder	1	uncertainty
		a suitcase or a heater	1	uncertainty
Shirt	10	on hanger; on fire extinguisher; on wall; hanging	6	co-location
		black	5	attribute
		long sleeves	2	attribute
		black thing hanging on wall (unclear what it is); black object	2	uncertainty
Sign	8	on the wall	4	co-location
		maybe indicating '3'?; roman numerals; 3 dashes; Arabic numbers; foreign language; room number 111	6	attribute
		poster	1	attribute
		map or blueprints	1	uncertainty
Green object	6	spherical	1	attribute
		hanging in window; in windowsill	2	co-location
		green thing outside room; green object; unidentifiable object; lime green object	4	uncertainty
		light post? fan?	1	uncertainty
Fire extinguisher	5	hanging off of black thing (also unclear as to what this is or does); on wall	3	co-location
		obscured	1	co-location
		cylindrical	1	attribute
		white and red thing; red object, white and red piece of object	3	uncertainty
Wall	4	wooden	1	attribute
		unfinished; visible plywood studs	2	unexpected
Bag	3	backpack or bag; something round; pile of clothes	2	uncertainty
		on the ground	2	co-location
		next to suitcase	1	co-location
Floor	2	marking of industry grade particle board, unfinished	2	attribute
Window	2			
Coat hanger	1	hanging on wall	1	co-location
		wire	1	attribute
		white	1	attribute
Shoes	1	shoes or hat	1	uncertainty
Rug	1			

Table 8: Object Identification for image$_2$

Object	#	Descriptor Text		#	Descriptor
Crockpot	7	on table		1	co-location
		green		2	attribute
		old fashioned		1	attribute
		kitchen appliance		1	attribute
		white or silver		1	uncertainty
Cereal box	7	on table		1	co-location
		to the right of crockpot		1	co-location
		shredded wheat		4	attribute
		cardboard		1	attribute
		printed black letters		1	attribute
Table	7	wood		3	attribute
		coffee table style		2	attribute
		pale		1	attribute
Pan	6	on ground; on floor		3	co-location
		blue handle		1	attribute
		medium-size		1	attribute
Container	5	clear		2	attribute
		plastic		3	attribute
		empty		2	attribute
		rectangular		1	attribute
		hinged top		1	attribute
Walls	2	lined with paper		1	attribute
Label	2	on pressure cooker		2	co-location
		white		1	attribute
Thread and needle	1	to the right of cereal box		1	co-location
Coffee pot	1	what looks like a coffee pot		1	uncertainty
		empty		1	attribute
		behind cereal box		1	attribute
Jam	1	plaid red and white lid		1	attribute
Door frame	1				

Table 9: Object Identification for image$_3$

Image	Single-Image Inferencing	Multi-Image Narration
Image$_1$	Someone sits at table and puts water bottle on floor while perhaps taking notes for others in some room. Folding chair suggests temporary or new use of space while building under construction.	
Image$_2$	Hallway view, suggesting exit path where someone might leave luggage while being in building	Same building as in the first scene because same type of wood for walls, floor, and opening/window construction. Arabic numbers on paper sign loosely attached (because wavy surface of paper e.g. not rigid, not laminated) to the wall suggests temporary designation of space for specific use, as an organized arrangement by some people for others.
Image$_3$	N/A	N/A

Table 10: A$_2$'s annotation

Image	Single-Image Inferencing	Multi-Image Narration
Image$_1$	I believe this is an office, because there is a computer monitor on a table, the table is serving as a desk, and there is a metal chair next to the monitor and the desk. A calendar is typically found in an office, however the calendar here is not in a location that is convenient for a person	
Image$_2$	I believe that this is a standard room that serves as a storage area. The absence of other objects does not hint at this room serving any other purpose.	I believe that this storage room is located in a home since personal items such as a luggage bag and spare shirt are not typically found in a public building. From the marked calendar in the previous picture, it appears that the occupants are preparing to travel very soon.
Image$_3$	N/A	N/A

Table 11: A$_3$'s annotation

Image	Single-Image Inferencing	Multi-Image Narration
Image₁	An office or computer setting/workstation. Actual computer maybe under desk (not visible) or missing. Water bottle suggests someone used this space recently. Chair not facing desk suggests person left in a hurry (not pushed under desk). Red circled date suggests some significance.	
Image₂	Shirt and suitcase suggests someone stored their personal items in this space. Room being labeled suggests recent occupants used more than 1 part of this space. Space does not look comfortable, but personal effects are here anyway. Holiday?	Someone camped out here and planned activities. They left in a hurry and didn't spend time putting things in their suitcases, or they had a visitor and the visitor left abruptly. The occupant may have left on the date marked in the calendar. The date may have had personal significance for an operation.
Image₃	N/A	N/A

Table 12: A_4's annotation

Image	Single-Image Inferencing	Multi-Image Narration
Image₁	Office (chair, desk, computer, calendar). Unfinished building (walls, floor, window)	
Image₂	In an unfinished building closet, common space. Things thrown to the side. Doesn't care much about office safety because fire extinguisher is covered, therefore not easily accessible.	Not sure about either workzone because randomly placed clothes and unsafe work environment. Could be a factory with unsafe conditions. Someone living or storing clothes in a "break room"?
Image₃	"Camp" site but not outdoors. Items on floor indicate some disarray or disregard for cleanliness. Why is the crock pot on the coffee table with cereal? Breakfast? But why are the walls strange?	Food like this shouldn't appear in a safe work environment, so I no longer think that. Someone seems to be living here in an unsafe and probably unregulated (re: fire extinguisher) way. Someone is hiding out in an uninhabited warehouse or work site (walls, floors, windows)

Table 13: A_5's annotation

Image	Single-Image Inferencing	Multi-Image Narration
Image₁	This is an office space because there is a desk, chair, computer and calendar. These items are typical items that would be in an office space.	
Image₂	This looks like a storage space, a closet, or the entrance/exit to a building. People typically pile things such as a suitcase, hanging clothes, backpack, etc. at one of those locations. A storage space or closet would allow for the items to be stored for a long time but would also be due to people being ready to leave on travel.	Due to the lack of decorations I would say these pictures were taken in a location where people were staying or working temporarily (like a headquarters safe house, etc.)
Image₃	These are items that would typically be found in a kitchen or break area. You would see a table or counter in a kitchen or break room. The pan and crock pot are not items that would be seen in other rooms, like a living room, office, bathroom, bedroom.	I would say this is a house or temporary space because the items are not organized and the surrounding area is not decorative. The scenes look messy and it doesn't look like it gets cleaned or has been cleaned recently. Plus the space contains a suitcase which gives the impressions that the person has not unpacked.

Table 14: A_6's annotation

Image	Single-Image Inferencing	Multi-Image Narration
Image$_1$	Looks like a place to work, with chair, table, monitor. Calendar is out of place because people don't have calendars from the edge of a table, so it can only be seen from the floor. Walls are unfurnished, only wood and plywood. A window in the wall, like an interior window. Not sure what it is a window for-why is the window in that location?	
Image$_2$	We are looking through a doorway or hallway. Shirt and suitcase belong together. Not sure what other objects are (green, red, black on ground).	Might be same location as Image 1, because the wooden/plywood walls and floor are similar. Not sure what the images have to do with each other, but might be 2 different rooms in same location. We're viewing this image from another room, because this room has a poster in it. Lighting of rooms is not very good, almost looks like spot lights, so not like an ordinary, prototypical house.
Image$_3$	A bunch of objects on a table, with a few objects underneath. The objects on/under the table all have to do with food or preparing food. Walls are light colored. In the foreground appears to be a wooden door jam. Although there are some kitchen items, this does not look like a typical kitchen	It is difficult to tell if this is in the same location as the previous 2 images. The wood door jam might be the same, but hard to know if wall is plywood and we don't see any other wooden framing. Rooms from all 3 images don't appear connected physically. No understandable context or connections.

Table 15: A$_7$'s annotation

Image	Single-Image Inferencing	Multi-Image Narration
Image$_1$	This looks like a make-shift room or space. Has a military of intel feel to it. Could be a briefing or an interrogation room. Given the prayer rug, definitely interaction between parties of different backgrounds, etc.	
Image$_2$	This view or room reflects living quarters. Given the nature of the condition of the wall, it is a make-shift. The existence of a number identifying this room indicates that it is one of many.	Combining the 2 pictures, this is beginning to look like part of a structure used for military/intel purposes. The location is most likely somewhere in the Middle East given how the numbers are written in Hindi indicating Arabic language. This also means we have multi-party/individual interactions.
Image$_3$	This picture has all the ingredients to presenting a kitchen: food and cookware leads to a kitchen. Given the "rough" look of the setting, this has the hallmarks of a make-shift kitchen.	This confirms, more than anything else, the scenario described in picture 2. As a whole, looks like some sort of post or output or a make-shift temporary type. Only necessities are present and the place couldn't quickly be abandoned.

Table 16: A$_9$'s annotation

Image	Single-Image Inferencing	Multi-Image Narration
Image$_1$	This was probably used as a workspace, given the chair and table with the monitor and the calendar. Someone was recently there because the bottle is upright.	
Image$_2$	This was a space that someone lived in given the clothes, fan(?), heater/suitcase(?). Given the mess, they left abruptly. The fire extinguisher indicates a presence because it is a safety aid.	This suggests we're in a space occupied by someone because of the office type and "living room" type room setup. It was purposefully made and left very abruptly (messy clothes, chair not pushed in).
Image$_3$	This seems to be a kitchen area because all objects are food related. It is messy. The rice cooker has a blue light and may be on. There is a window letting in light, visible on the back wall.	This supports the assumption that the environment was recently occupied. Food is opened, rice cooker is on, mess suggests it was abruptly abandoned, much like image 2's mess. The robot appears to be I the doorway at an angle.

Table 17: A$_{10}$'s annotation

Telling Stories with Soundtracks: An Empirical Analysis of Music in Film

Jon Gillick
School of Information
University of California, Berkeley
jongillick@berkeley.edu

David Bamman
School of Information
University of California, Berkeley
dbamman@berkeley.edu

Abstract

Soundtracks play an important role in carrying the story of a film. In this work, we collect a corpus of movies and television shows matched with subtitles and soundtracks and analyze the relationship between story, song, and audience reception. We look at the content of a film through the lens of its latent topics and at the content of a song through descriptors of its musical attributes. In two experiments, we find first that individual topics are strongly associated with musical attributes, and second, that musical attributes of soundtracks are predictive of film ratings, even after controlling for topic and genre.

1 Introduction

The medium of film is often taken to be a canonical example of narrative multimodality: it combines the written narrative of dialogue with the visual narrative of its imagery. While words bear the burden alone for creating compelling characters, scenes, and plot in textual narratives like literary novels, in film, this responsibility is shared by each of the contributors, including the screenwriter, director, music supervisor, special effects engineers, and many others. Working together to support the overall story tends to make for more successful component parts; the Academy Award winner for Best Picture, for example, often also collects many other awards and nominations—including acting, cinemotography, and sound design.

While film has recently been studied as a target in natural language processing and computer vision for such tasks as characterizing gender representation in dialogue (Ramakrishna et al., 2015; Agarwal et al., 2015), inferring character types from plot summaries (Bamman et al., 2013), measuring the memorability of phrasing (Danescu-Niculescu-Mizil et al., 2012), question answering (Guha et al., 2015; Kočiský et al., 2017), natural language understanding (Frermann et al., 2017), summarization (Gorinski and Lapata, 2015) and image captioning (Zhu et al., 2015; Rohrbach et al., 2015, 2017; Tapaswi et al., 2015), the modalities examined are almost exclusively limited to text and image. In this work, we present a new perspective on multimodal storytelling by focusing on a so-far neglected aspect of narrative: the role of music.

We focus specifically on the ways in which soundtracks contribute to films,[1] presenting a first look from a computational modeling perspective into soundtracks as storytelling devices. By developing models that connect films with musical parameters of soundtracks, we can gain insight into musical choices both past and future. While a great film score is in part determined by how well it fits with the context of the story (Byrne, 2012), we are also interested in uncovering musical aspects that, in general, work better *in support of a film*.

To move toward understanding both what makes a film fit with a particular kind of song and what musical aspects can broadly be effective in the service of telling a story, we make the following contributions:

1. We present a dataset of 41,143 films paired with their soundtracks. Metadata for the films is drawn from IMDB, linked to subtitle information from OpenSubtitles2016 data (Lison and Tiedemann, 2016), and soundtrack data is linked to structured audio information from Spotify.

2. We present empirical results demonstrating the relationship between audio qualities of the soundtrack and viewers' responses to

---

[1]We use the word *film* to refer to both movies and television shows interchangeably.

Proceedings of the First Workshop on Storytelling, pages 33–42
New Orleans, Louisiana, June 5, 2018. ©2018 Association for Computational Linguistics

the films they appear in; soundtracks with more instrumental or acoustic songs generate higher ratings; "danceable" songs lower the average ratings for films they appear in.

3. We present empirical results demonstrating the relationship between the topics that make up a film script and the audio qualities of the soundtrack. Films with settings in high school or college, for example, tend to have electric instrumentation and singing; soundtracks with faster tempos appear both in films about zombies and vampires and in films in which the word *dude* appears frequently.

2 The Narrative Role of Music in Film

The first films appeared around 1890, before the development of technology that enabled synchronization of picture with sound (Buhler et al., 2010). While silent films featured no talking or music in the film itself, they were often accompanied by music during live performances in theatres. Rather than playing set scores, these live accompaniments were largely improvised; practical catalogues for such performances describe the musical elements appropriate for emotions and narrative situations in the film (Becce, 1919; Erdmann et al., 1927). For example, Lang and West (1920) note that a string accompaniment with tremolo (trembling) effect is appropriate for "suspense and impending disaster"; an organ tone with heavy pedal is appropriate for "church scenes" and for generally connoting "impressive dignity"; flutes are fitting for conveying "happiness," "springtime" or "sunshine."

With the rise of talkies in the late 1920's (Slowik, 2012), music could be incorporated directly into the production of the film, and was often composed specifically for it; Gorbman (1987) describes that in the classical model of film production, scored music is "not meant to be heard consciously," primarily acts as a signifier of emotion, and provides referential and narrative cues, such as establishing the setting or character. The use of Wagnerian leitmotif—the repeated association of a musical phrase with a film element, such as a character—is common in original scores, especially in those for epic films (Prendergast, 1992).

Works from the "Golden Age" of film music (the period between 1935–1950, shortly after the rise of synchronized sound) set the standard for cinematic scoring practices and have been extensively analyzed in the film music literature (Slowik, 2012). Following this period, with the rise of rock and roll, popular music began to make its way into film soundtracks in addition to the scores written specifically for the movie. As Rodman (2006) points out, this turn coincided with directors seeing the potential for songs to contribute to the narrative meaning of the film:

> In *The Blackboard Jungle*, Bill Haley's rock and roll anthem, 'Rock Around the Clock,' was used in the opening credits, not only to capture the attention of the teenage audience, but also to signify the rebellious energy of teenagers in the 1950s. . . . *The Graduate* relied upon the music and poetry of Simon and Garfunkel to portray the alienation of American youth of the 1960s. *Easy Rider* took a more aggressive countercultural stance by using the rock music of Hoyt Axton, Steppenwolf, The Byrds, and Jimi Hendrix to portray the youth rebellion in American society, complete with communes, long hair and drugs (Rodman, 2006, 123)

In recent years, the boundaries between popular music and film music in the traditional sense have become increasingly blurred, pushed forward especially by more affordable music production technology including synthesizers and prerecorded samples that allow a broad range of composers to use sounds previously reserved for those with access to a full orchestra (Pinch et al., 2009). Though electronic music pioneers like Wendy Carlos have been composing for film since the late 1960's (Pinch et al., 2009), pop and electronic musicians have only gradually been recognized as film composers in their own right, with Daft Punk's original score for *Tron: Legacy* in 2010 marking a breakthrough into the mainstream (Anderson, 2012).

3 Data

In order to begin exploring the relationship between films and their soundtracks, we gather data from several different sources. First, we draw on the OpenSubtitles2016 data of parallel texts for film subtitles (Lison and Tiedemann, 2016); this dataset includes scripts for a wide variety of movies and episodes of television shows (106,609 total in English) and contains publicly available subtitle data. Each film in the OpenSubtitles2016 data is paired with its unique IMDB identifier; using this information, we extract IMDB metadata for the film, including title, year of release, average user rating (a real number from 0-10), and genre (a set of 28 categories, ranging from drama and comedy to war and film-noir).

Most importantly, we also identify soundtrack information on IMDB using this identifier; soundtracks are listed on IMDB in the same form as they appear in the movie/television credits (generally also in the order of appearance of the song). A typical example is the following:

> Golden Slumbers
> Written by John Lennon and Paul McCartney
> Performed by Jennifer Hudson
> Jennifer Hudson appears courtesy of Epic Records
> Produced by Harvey Mason Jr.

This structured format is very consistent across films (owing to the codification of the appearance of this information in a film's closing credits, which is thereby preserved in the user transcription on IMDB[2]). For each song in a soundtrack for a film, we extract the title, performers and writers through regular expressions (which are precise given the structured format).

We then identify target candidate matches for a source soundtrack song by querying the public Spotify API for all target songs in the Spotify catalogue with the same title as the source song in the IMDB soundtrack. The names of performers are not standardized across datasets (e.g., IMDB may list an artist as *The Velvet Underground*, while Spotify may list the same performance as *The Velvet Underground and Nico*). To account for this, we identify exact matches between songs as those that share the same title and where the longest common substring between the source and target performers spans at least 75% the length of either entity; if no exact match is found, we identify the best secondary match as the target song with the highest Spotify popularity among target candidates with the same title as the source. In the example above, if this particular performance

of *Golden Slumbers* by Jennifer Hudson (from the movie *Sing*) were not in Spotify's catalogue, it would match the performance by The Beatles on *Abbey Road*.

Spotify provides a number of extracted audio features for each song; from a set of 13 we chose 5 that we hypothesized would be predictive of viewer preferences and whose descriptors are also interpretable enough to enable discussion. Those that we include in our analysis are the following, with descriptions drawn from Spotify's Track API:[3]

- **Mode**. "Mode indicates the modality (major or minor) of a track, the type of scale from which its melodic content is derived. Major is represented by 1 and minor is 0."

- **Tempo**. "The overall estimated tempo of a track in beats per minute (BPM). In musical terminology, tempo is the speed or pace of a given piece and derives directly from the average beat duration." In the raw data, these range from 36 to 240; we divide by the maximum value of 240 to give a range between 0.15 and 1.

- **Danceability**. "Danceability describes how suitable a track is for dancing based on a combination of musical elements including tempo, rhythm stability, beat strength, and overall regularity. A value of 0.0 is least danceable and 1.0 is most danceable."

- **Instrumentalness**. "Instrumentalness predicts whether a track contains no vocals. 'Ooh' and 'aah' sounds are treated as instrumental in this context. Rap or spoken word tracks are clearly 'vocal.' The closer the instrumentalness value is to 1.0, the greater likelihood the track contains no vocal content. Values above 0.5 are intended to represent instrumental tracks, but confidence is higher as the value approaches 1.0."

- **Acousticness**. "A confidence measure from 0.0 to 1.0 of whether the track is acoustic. 1.0 represents high confidence the track is acoustic."

The dataset totals 189,340 songs (96,526 unique) from 41,143 movies/television shows,

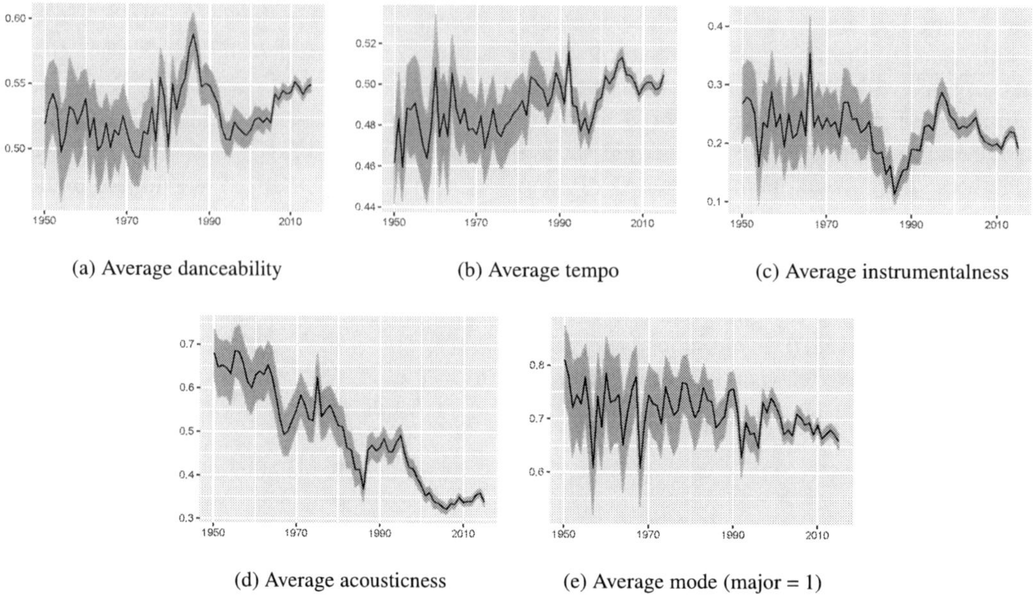

(a) Average danceability   (b) Average tempo   (c) Average instrumentalness

(d) Average acousticness   (e) Average mode (major = 1)

Figure 1: Change in audio features over time, 1950–2015. Films and TV shows in the late 1980s peaked for danceable soundtracks, with electric instrumentation and singing. Each plot displays the average value for that feature, with 95% bootstrap confidence intervals.

along with a paired script for each movie/show. Figures 1 and 2 provide summary statistics of this dataset (using only the metadata and audio features) and begin to demonstrate the potential of this data. Figure 1 illustrates the change in the average value of each feature between 1950–2015. Soundtracks featuring acoustic songs naturally decline over this time period with the rise of electric instruments; as time progresses, soundtracks feature quicker tempos and include more songs in minor keys. The 1980s in particular are peaks for danceable soundtracks, with electric instrumentation and voice, while the 1990s appear to react against this dominance by featuring songs with comparatively lower danceability, higher acoustic instrumentation, and less singing.

Figure 2, in contrast, displays variations in selected audio features across genres. Movies and television shows tagged by IMDB users with genre labels of "war" and "western" tend to have songs that are slow and in major keys, whereas game shows and adult films more often have faster songs in minor keys. We can also see from figure 2 that different audio characteristics can have different amounts of variation across genres; mode varies more with genre than tempo does.

4 Analysis

We present two analyses here shedding some light on the role that music plays in the narrative form of films, demonstrating the relationship between fine-grained topics in a film's script and specific audio features described in §3 above; and measure the impact of audio features in the soundtrack on the *reception* to the storytelling in the form of user reviews, attempting to control for the topical and generic influence of the script using topically-coarsened exact matching in causal inference (Roberts et al., 2016).

4.1 Topic analysis of audio features

While we can expect to see trends in the music employed in films over time and across genres, these surface descriptors do not tell us about the actual *contents* of the film. What kind of stories have soundtracks in minor keys? Is there a relationship between the content of a movie or television show and the tempo of its soundtrack? We investigate this by regressing the content of the script against each audio feature; rather than representing the script by the individual words it contains, we seek instead to uncover the relationship between broad thematic topics implicit in the script and those fea-

36

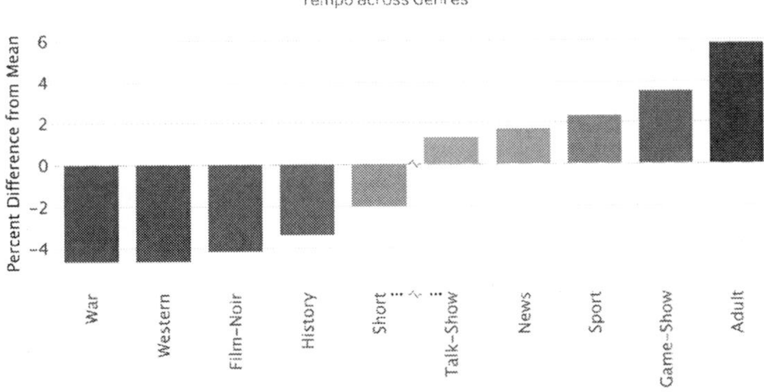

(a) Top and bottom 5 film genres with the fastest and slowest soundtracks. Blue indicates faster tempos and red indicates slower tempos.

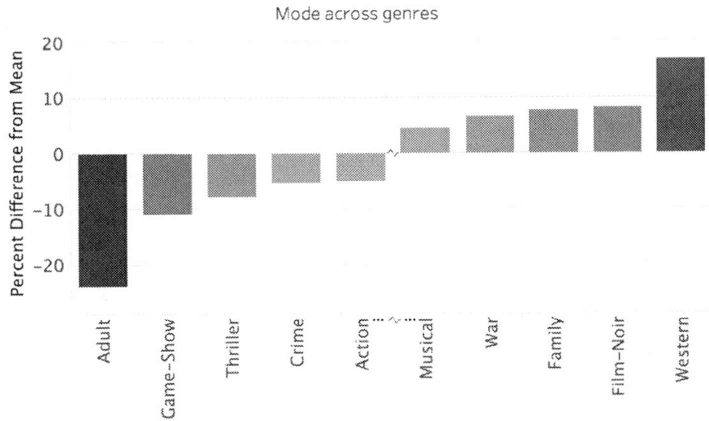

(b) Top and bottom 5 film genres whose soundtracks are most major and most minor. Blue indicates major and red indicates minor.

Figure 2: Top and bottom 5 film genres in terms of average tempo and mode. Heights of the bars represent percentage difference from the mean across the entire dataset. Actual values are at the tops of the bars.

tures.

To do so, we identify topics in all 41,143 scripts using LDA (Blei et al., 2003), modeling each script as a distribution over 50 inferred topics, removing stopwords and names.

We model the impact of individual topics on audio features by representing each document as its 50-dimensional distribution of topic proportions; in order to place both very frequent and infrequent topics on the same scale, we normalize each topic to a standard normal across the dataset. For each of the four real-valued audio features $y = \{danceability, acousticness, instrumentalness,$ and $tempo\}$, we regress the relationship between the document-topic representations in turn using OLS; for the binary-valued *mode* variable (major vs. minor key), we model the relationship between the topic representations using binary logistic regression.

Table 1 illustrates the five strongest positive and negative topic predictors for each audio feature.

While the latent topics do not have defined categories, we can extract salient aspects of the stories based on the words in the most prevalent topics. The words describing the topics most and least associated with an audio feature can give us some insight into how songs are used in soundtracks.

- **Mode**. Major versus minor is typically one of the most stark musical contrasts, with the major key being characteristically associated with joy and excitement, and the minor key being associated with melancholy (Hevner, 1935). We see songs in major being used in

0.141	captain ship sir	0.044	mr. sir mrs.	0.017	baby yo y'all
0.074	town horse sheriff	0.028	boy huh big	0.010	woman married sex
0.055	sir colonel planet	0.020	christmas la aa	0.008	sir brother heart
0.050	boy huh big	0.019	sir dear majesty	0.007	dude cool whoa
0.050	mr. sir mrs.	0.019	leave understand father	0.006	spanish el la
-0.045	sir brother heart	-0.017	um work fine	-0.006	father lord church
-0.052	leave understand father	-0.018	kill dead blood	-0.007	remember feel dead
-0.054	gibbs mcgee boss	-0.020	fuck shit fucking	-0.008	sir dear majesty
-0.066	agent security phone	-0.021	school class college	-0.011	captain ship sir
-0.083	baby yo y'all	-0.024	dude cool whoa	-0.015	sir colonel planet

(a) mode (major/minor)   (b) acousticness   (c) danceability

0.003	dude cool whoa	0.025	sir colonel planet
0.003	sir colonel planet	0.020	mr. sir mrs.
0.002	music show sing	0.017	years world work
0.002	um work fine	0.017	captain ship sir
0.002	kill dead blood	0.016	agent security phone
-0.002	baby yo y'all	-0.011	school class college
-0.002	remember feel dead	-0.012	baby yo y'all
-0.002	sir dear majesty	-0.013	woman married sex
-0.004	mr. sir mrs.	-0.014	sir brother heart
-0.005	captain ship sir	-0.015	music show sing

(d) tempo   (e) instrumentalness

Table 1: Script topics predictive of audio features. For each feature, the 5 topics most predictive of high feature values (1-5) and the 5 topics most predictive of low feature values (46-50) are shown. Topics are displayed as the top three most frequent words within them. Coefficients for mode (as a categorical variable) are for binary logistic regression; those for all other features are for linear regression.

films with polite greetings, those with sheriffs and horses, and with ship captains. Minor songs appear more often in stories involving separation from parents, FBI agents, or viruses. The strongest topic associated with major key is *"captain ship"*; productions mostly strongly associated with this topic include episodes from the TV show *Star Trek: The Next Generation*.

- **Acousticness**. The acousticness of a soundtrack captures the degree of electric instrumentation; as figure 4(d) shows, acousticness shows the greatest decline over time (corresponding to the rise of electric instruments); we see this also reflected topically here, with the topic most strongly associated with acoustic soundtracks being *"mr. sir mrs."*; this topic tends to appear in period pieces and older films, such as *Arsenic and Old Lace* (1944).

- **Danceability**. The danceability of a song is the degree to which is it suitable for dancing. The topics most strongly associated with consistently danceable soundtracks including

"baby yo"—dominant in movies like *Malibu's Most Wanted* (2003), *Menace II Society* (1993) *Hustle & Flow* (2005)—and *"women married"*—dominant in episodes of *Friends* and *Sex and the City*.

- **Tempo**. Musical tempo is a measure of pace; the strongest topic associated with fast pace is the *"dude cool"* topic, include episodes from the TV show *Workaholics* and *The Simpsons*. Perhaps unsurprisingly, the mannered *"mr. sir mrs."* topic is associated with a slow tempo.

- **Instrumentalness**. Instrumentalness measures the degree to which a song is entirely instrumental (i.e., devoid of vocals like singing), such as classical music. The *"mr. sir mrs."* topic again rates highly along this dimension (presumably corresponding with the use of classical music in these films); also highly ranking is the *"sir colonel"* topic, which is primarily a subgenre of science fiction, including episodes from the TV show *Stargate* and the movie *Star Wars: Episode III: Revenge of the Sith* (2005).

4.2 Impact on ratings

While the analysis above examines the internal relationship between a film's soundtrack and its narrative, we can also explore the relationship between the soundtrack and a film's reception: how do audiences respond to movies with fast soundtracks, to acoustic soundtracks, or to soundtracks that are predominantly classical (i.e., with high instrumentalness)? We measure response in this work by the average user rating for the film on IMDB (a real value from 0-10).

One confound with this kind of analysis is the complication with the content of the script; as §4.1 demonstrates, some topics are clearly associated with audio features like "acousticness," so if we identify a relationship between acousticness and a film's rating, that might simply be a relationship between the underlying topic (e.g., *"dude,"* *"cool,"* *"whoa"*) and the rating, rather than acousticness in itself.

In order to account for this, we employ methods from causal inference in observational studies, drawing on the methods of coarsened exact matching using topic distributions developed by Roberts et al. (2016). Conventional methods for exact matching aim to identify the latent causal experiment lurking within observational data by eliminating all sources of variation in covariates except for the variable of interest, identifying a subset of the original data in which covariates are balanced between treatment conditions; in our case, if 100 films have high tempo, 100 have low tempo and the 200 films are identical in every other dimension, then if tempo has a significant correlation with a film's rating, we can interpret that significance causally (since there is no other source of variation to explain the relationship).

True causal inference is dependent on accurate model specification (e.g., its assumptions fail if an important explanatory covariate is omitted). In our case, we are seeking to model the relationship between audio features of the soundtrack and IMDB reviewers' average rating for a film, and include features representing the content of a film through a.) its topic distribution and b.) explicit genre categories from IMDB (a binary value for each of the 28 genres). We know that this model is mis-specified—surely other factors of a film's content impacting its rating may also be correlated with audio features—but in using the machinery of causal inference, we seek not to make causal claims but rather to provide a stricter criterion against which to assess the significance of our results.

Here, let us define the "treatment variable" to be the variable (such as "acousticness") whose relationship with rating we are seeking to establish. The original value for this variable is real; we binarize it into two treatment conditions (0 and 1) by thresholding at 0.5 (all values above this limit are set to 1; otherwise 0). To test the relationship between audio features and user ratings in this procedure, we place each data point in a stratum defined by the values of its other covariates; we coarsen the values of each covariate into a binary value: for all numeric audio features, we binarize at a threshold of 0.5; for topic distributions, we coarsen by selecting the argmax topic as the single binary topic value. For each stratum with at least 5 data points in each treatment condition, we sample data points to reflect the overall distribution of the treatment variable in the data; any data points in strata for which there are fewer than 5 points from each condition are excluded from analysis. This, across all strata, defines our matched data for analysis. We carry out this process once for each treatment variable {*mode, danceability, acousticness, instrumentalness,* and *tempo*}.

Coefficient	Audio feature
0.121*	Acousticness
0.117*	Instrumentalness
0.031	Tempo
0.024*	Mode
−0.103*	Danceability

Table 2: Impact of audio features on IMDB average user rating. Features marked * are significant at $p \leq 0.001$.

Table 2 presents the results of this analysis: all audio features of the soundtrack except tempo have a significant (if small) impact on the average user rating for the film they appear with. A highly danceable soundtrack would lower the score of a film from 9.0 to a 8.897; adding an acoustic soundtrack would raise it to 9.121; and adding an instrumental soundtrack with no vocals would raise it to 9.117. Our experiments suggest that certain musical aspects might be generally more effective than others in the context of a film score, and that these attributes significantly shape a viewer's reactions to the overall film.

5 Previous Work

Because the ability to forecast box office success is of practical interest for studios who want to decide which scripts to "Greenlight" (Eliashberg et al., 2007; Joshi et al., 2010) or where to invest marketing dollars (Mestyán et al., 2013), a number of previous studies look at predicting movie success by measuring box office revenue or viewer ratings. Eliashberg et al. (2007) used linear regression on metadata and textual features drawn from "spoilers", detailed summaries written by moviegoers, to predict return on investment in movie-making. Joshi et al. (2010) used review text from critics to predict revenues, finding n-gram and dependency relation features to informative complement to metadata-based features. Jain (2013) used Twitter sentiment to predict box office revenue, further classifying movies as either a Hit, a Flop, or Average. Oghina et al. (2012) used features computed from Twitter and YouTube comments to predict IMDB ratings.

Though a number of previous works have attempted to predict film performance from text and metadata, little attention has been paid to the role of the soundtrack in a movie's success. Xu and Goonawardene (2014) did consider soundtracks, finding the volume of internet searches for a movie's soundtrack preceding a release to be predictive of box office revenue. This work, however, only considers the popularity of the soundtrack as a surface feature; it does not directly measure whether the *musical characteristics* of the songs in the soundtracks are themselves predictive.

6 Conclusion

In this work, we introduce a new dataset of films, subtitles, and soundtracks along with two empirical analyses, the first demonstrating the connections between the contents of a story, (as measured by the topics in its script) and the musical features that make up its soundtrack, and the second identifying musical aspects that are associated with better user ratings on IMDB. Soundtracks using acoustic instruments, as measured by Spotify's "acousticness" descriptor, and those with instruments but no vocals, as measured by the "instrumentalness" descriptor, are each linked with more than a 0.11 increase in ratings on a 10-star scale, even when controlling for other musical dimensions, topic, and genre through Coarsened Exact Matching. Soundtracks that are more "danceable"

point in the opposite direction, indicating a decrease of 0.1 stars.

We hope that one of the primary beneficiaries of the line of work introduced here will be *music supervisors*, whose job involves choosing existing music to license or hiring composers to create original scores. Understanding the connections between the different modalities that contribute to a story can be useful for understanding the history of film scoring and music licensing as well as for making decisions during the production process. Though traditionally the music supervisor plays a well-defined role on a film, in contemporary practice many people contribute to music supervision throughout the production process for all kinds of media, from movies and television to advertising, social media, and games.

There are several directions of future research that are worth further pursuit. First, while we have shown that strong relationships exist between films and their soundtracks as a whole and that a soundtrack is predictive of user ratings, this relationship only obtains over the entirety of the script and the entirety of the soundtrack; a more fine-grained model would anchor occurrences of individual songs at specific moments in the temporal narrative of the script. While our data does not directly indicate *when* a song occurs, latent variable modeling over the scripts and soundtracks in our collection may provide a reasonable path forward. Second, while our work here has focused on descriptive analysis of this new data, a potentially powerful application is *soundtrack generation*: creating a new soundtrack for a film given the input of a script. This application has the potential to be useful for music supervisors, by suggesting candidate songs that fit the narrative of a given script in production.

Music is a vital storytelling component of multimodal narratives such as film, television and theatre, and we hope to drive further work in this area. Data and code to support this work can be found at `https://github.com/jrgillick/music_supervisor`.

7 Acknowledgments

Many thanks to the anonymous reviewers for their helpful feedback. The research reported in this article was supported by a UC Berkeley Fellowship for Graduate Study to J.G.

References

Apoorv Agarwal, Jiehan Zheng, Shruti Kamath, Sriramkumar Balasubramanian, and Shirin Ann Dey. 2015. Key female characters in film have more to talk about besides men: Automating the bechdel test. In *Proceedings of the 2015 Conference of the North American Chapter of the Association for Computational Linguistics: Human Language Technologies*. Association for Computational Linguistics, Denver, Colorado, pages 830–840. http://www.aclweb.org/anthology/N15-1084.

Stacey Anderson. 2012. Electronic dance music goes hollywood. *The New York Times* .

David Bamman, Brendan O'Connor, and Noah A. Smith. 2013. Learning latent personas of film characters. In *Proceedings of the 51st Annual Meeting of the Association for Computational Linguistics (Volume 1: Long Papers)*. Association for Computational Linguistics, Sofia, Bulgaria, pages 352–361.

Giuseppe Becce, editor. 1919. *Kinothek. Neue Filmmusik*. Schlesinger'sche Buchhandlung.

David M. Blei, Andrew Ng, and Michael Jordan. 2003. Latent dirichlet allocation. *JMLR* 3:993–1022.

James Buhler, David Neumeyer, and Rob Deemer. 2010. *Hearing the movies: music and sound in film history*. Oxford University Press New York.

David Byrne. 2012. *How music works*. Three Rivers Press.

Cristian Danescu-Niculescu-Mizil, Justin Cheng, Jon Kleinberg, and Lillian Lee. 2012. You had me at hello: How phrasing affects memorability. In *Proceedings of the 50th Annual Meeting of the Association for Computational Linguistics: Long Papers - Volume 1*. Association for Computational Linguistics, Stroudsburg, PA, USA, ACL '12, pages 892–901. http://dl.acm.org/citation.cfm?id=2390524.2390647.

Jehoshua Eliashberg, Sam K Hui, and Z John Zhang. 2007. From story line to box office: A new approach for green-lighting movie scripts. *Management Science* 53(6):881–893.

Hans Erdmann, Giuseppe Becce, and Ludwig Brav. 1927. *Allgemeines Handbuch der Film-Musik*. Schlesinger.

Lea Frermann, Shay B Cohen, and Mirella Lapata. 2017. Whodunnit? crime drama as a case for natural language understanding. *arXiv preprint arXiv:1710.11601* .

Claudia Gorbman. 1987. *Unheard melodies: Narrative film music*. Indiana University Press.

Philip John Gorinski and Mirella Lapata. 2015. Movie script summarization as graph-based scene extraction. In *Proceedings of the 2015 Conference of the North American Chapter of the Association for Computational Linguistics: Human Language Technologies*. pages 1066–1076.

Tanaya Guha, Che-Wei Huang, Naveen Kumar, Yan Zhu, and Shrikanth S Narayanan. 2015. Gender representation in cinematic content: A multimodal approach. In *Proceedings of the 2015 ACM on International Conference on Multimodal Interaction*. ACM, pages 31–34.

Kate Hevner. 1935. The affective character of the major and minor modes in music. *The American Journal of Psychology* 47(1):103–118. http://www.jstor.org/stable/1416710.

Vasu Jain. 2013. Prediction of movie success using sentiment analysis of tweets. *The International Journal of Soft Computing and Software Engineering* 3(3):308–313.

Mahesh Joshi, Dipanjan Das, Kevin Gimpel, and Noah A Smith. 2010. Movie reviews and revenues: An experiment in text regression. In *Human Language Technologies: The 2010 Annual Conference of the North American Chapter of the Association for Computational Linguistics*. Association for Computational Linguistics, pages 293–296.

Tomáš Kočiskỳ, Jonathan Schwarz, Phil Blunsom, Chris Dyer, Karl Moritz Hermann, Gábor Melis, and Edward Grefenstette. 2017. The narrativeqa reading comprehension challenge. *arXiv preprint arXiv:1712.07040* .

Edith Lang and George West. 1920. *Musical accompaniment of moving pictures; a practical manual for pianists and organists and an exposition of the principles underlying the musical interpretation of moving pictures, by*. The Boston Music Co., Boston.

Pierre Lison and Jrg Tiedemann. 2016. Opensubtitles2016: Extracting large parallel corpora from movie and tv subtitles. In Nicoletta Calzolari (Conference Chair), Khalid Choukri, Thierry Declerck, Sara Goggi, Marko Grobelnik, Bente Maegaard, Joseph Mariani, Helene Mazo, Asuncion Moreno, Jan Odijk, and Stelios Piperidis, editors, *Proceedings of the Tenth International Conference on Language Resources and Evaluation (LREC 2016)*. European Language Resources Association (ELRA), Paris, France.

Márton Mestyán, Taha Yasseri, and János Kertész. 2013. Early prediction of movie box office success based on wikipedia activity big data. *PloS one* 8(8):e71226.

Andrei Oghina, Mathias Breuss, Manos Tsagkias, and Maarten de Rijke. 2012. Predicting imdb movie ratings using social media. In *European Conference on Information Retrieval*. Springer, pages 503–507.

Trevor J Pinch, Frank Trocco, and TJ Pinch. 2009. *Analog days: The invention and impact of the Moog synthesizer*. Harvard University Press.

Roy M Prendergast. 1992. *Film music: a neglected art: a critical study of music in films*. WW Norton & Company.

Anil Ramakrishna, Nikolaos Malandrakis, Elizabeth Staruk, and Shrikanth Narayanan. 2015. A quantitative analysis of gender differences in movies using psycholinguistic normatives. In *Proceedings of the 2015 Conference on Empirical Methods in Natural Language Processing*. Association for Computational Linguistics, Lisbon, Portugal, pages 1996–2001. https://aclweb.org/anthology/D/D15/D15-1234.

Margaret E. Roberts, Brandon Stewart, and R. Nielsen. 2016. Matching methods for high-dimensional data with applications to text. Working paper.

Ronald Rodman. 2006. The popular song as leitmotif in 1990s film. *Changing Tunes: The Use of Pre-existing Music in Film* pages 119–136.

Anna Rohrbach, Marcus Rohrbach, Niket Tandon, and Bernt Schiele. 2015. A dataset for movie description. *CVPR* .

Anna Rohrbach, Atousa Torabi, Marcus Rohrbach, Niket Tandon, Christopher Pal, Hugo Larochelle, Aaron Courville, and Bernt Schiele. 2017. Movie description. *International Journal of Computer Vision* 123(1):94–120. https://doi.org/10.1007/s11263-016-0987-1.

Michael James Slowik. 2012. Hollywood film music in the early sound era, 1926-1934 .

Makarand Tapaswi, Martin Bauml, and Rainer Stiefelhagen. 2015. Book2movie: Aligning video scenes with book chapters. In *The IEEE Conference on Computer Vision and Pattern Recognition (CVPR)*.

Haifeng Xu and Nadee Goonawardene. 2014. Does movie soundtrack matter? the role of soundtrack in predicting movie revenue. In *PACIS*. page 350.

Yukun Zhu, Ryan Kiros, Richard S. Zemel, Ruslan Salakhutdinov, Raquel Urtasun, Antonio Torralba, and Sanja Fidler. 2015. Aligning books and movies: Towards story-like visual explanations by watching movies and reading books. *ICCV* .

Towards Controllable Story Generation

Nanyun Peng   Marjan Ghazvininejad   Jonathan May   Kevin Knight
Information Sciences Institute & Computer Science Department
University of Southern California
{npeng,ghazvini,jonmay,knight}@isi.edu

Abstract

We present a general framework of analyzing existing story corpora to generate controllable and creative new stories. The proposed framework needs little manual annotation to achieve controllable story generation. It creates a new interface for humans to interact with computers to generate personalized stories. We apply the framework to build recurrent neural network (RNN)-based generation models to control story ending valence[1] (Egidi and Gerrig, 2009) and storyline. Experiments show that our methods successfully achieve the control and enhance the coherence of stories through introducing storylines. with additional control factors, the generation model gets lower perplexity, and yields more coherent stories that are faithful to the control factors according to human evaluation.

1   Introduction

Storytelling is an important task in natural language generation, which plays a crucial role in the generation of various types of texts, such as novels, movies, and news articles. Automatic story generation efforts started as early as the 1970s with the TALE-SPIN system (Meehan, 1977). Early attempts in this field relied on symbolic planning (Meehan, 1977; Lebowitz, 1987; Turner, 1993; Bringsjord and Ferrucci, 1999; Perez and Sharples, 2001; Riedl and Young, 2010), case-based reasoning (Gervas et al., 2005), or generalizing knowledge from existing stories to assemble new ones (Swanson and Gordon, 2012; Li et al., 2013). In recent years, deep learning models are used to capture higher level structure in stories. Roemmele et al. (2017) use skip-thought vectors (Kiros et al., 2015) to encode sentences, and a Long Short-Term Memory (LSTM) network (Hochreiter and Schmidhuber, 1997) to gen-

---

[1]Happy or sad endings.

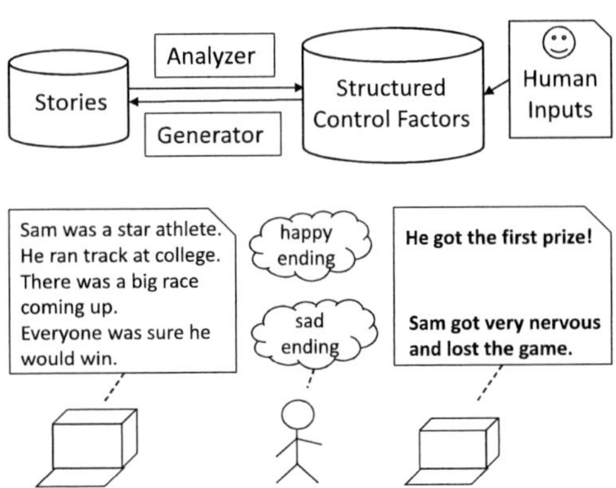

Figure 1:   An overview (upper) and an example (lower) of the proposed analyze-to-generate story framework.

erate stories. Martin et al. (2017) train a recurrent encoder-decoder neural network (Sutskever et al., 2014) to predict the next event in the story.

Despite significant progress in automatic story generation, there has been less emphasis on *controllability*: having a system takes human inputs and composes stories accordingly. With the recent successes on controllable generation of images (Chen et al., 2016; Siddharth et al., 2017; Lample et al., 2017), dialog responses (Wang et al., 2017), poems (Ghazvininejad et al., 2017), and different styles of text (Hu et al., 2017; Ficler and Goldberg, 2017; Shen et al., 2017; Fu et al., 2017). people would want to control a story generation system to produce interesting and personalized stories.

This paper emphasizes the *controllability* aspect. We propose a completely data-driven approach towards controllable story generation by analyzing the existing story corpora. First, an analyzer extracts control factors from existing stories, and then a generator learns to generate stories according to the control factors. This creates an excellent interface for humans to interact: the generator can take human-supplied control factors to generate stories that reflect a user's intent. Fig-

43

Proceedings of the First Workshop on Storytelling, pages 43–49
New Orleans, Louisiana, June 5, 2018. ©2018 Association for Computational Linguistics

ure 1 gives the overview (upper) and an example (lower) of the framework. The instantiations of the analyzer and the generator are flexible and can be easily applied to different scenarios. We explore two control factors: (1) ending valence (happy or sad ending) and (2) storyline keywords. We use supervised classifiers and rule-based keyword extractors for analysis, and conditional RNNs for generation.

The contributions of the paper are two-fold:

1. We propose a general framework enabling interactive story generation by analyzing existing story corpora.

2. We apply the framework to control story ending valence and storyline, and show that with these additional control factors, our models generate stories that are both more coherent and more faithful to human inputs.

2 Controllable Story Generation

As a pilot study, we explore the control of 1) ending valence, which is an abstract, style-level element of stories, and 2) storyline, which is a more concrete, content-level concept for stories.

2.1 Ending Valence Control

Prior work has explored manipulating emotion in interactive storytelling (Cavazza et al., 2009). For simplicity, we refine our scope to manipulating the ending valence for controllable story generation. We categorize ending valence into *happyEnding, sadEnding*, or *cannotTell*.

Analyzer. The analyzer for the ending valence control is a *classifier* that labels each story as *happyEnding, sadEnding*, or *cannotTell*. Formally, given a story corpus $X = \{\mathbf{x}_1, \mathbf{x}_2, \cdots, \mathbf{x}_N\}$ with N stories, the ending valence analyzer is a function f^v that maps each story $\mathbf{x}_i$ to a label l_i:

$$l_i = f^v(\mathbf{x}_i),$$

where i indexes instances. Since there is no prior work on analyzing story ending valence, we build our own analyzer by collecting some annotations for story ending valence from Amazon Mechanical Turk (AMT) and building a supervised classifier. We employ an LSTM-based logistic regression classifier as it learns feature representations that capture long-term dependencies between the words, and has been shown efficient in text classification tasks (Tang et al., 2015).

Specifically, we use a bidirectional-LSTM to encode an input story into a sequence of vector representations $\mathbf{h}_i = \{h_{i,1}, h_{i,2}, \cdots, h_{i,T}\}$, where $\mathbf{h_i} = BiLSTM(\mathbf{x}_i) = [\overrightarrow{\mathbf{h}}_i; \overleftarrow{\mathbf{h}}_i]$, T denotes the story length, $[,:,]$ denotes element-wise concatenation. $\overrightarrow{\mathbf{h}}_i$ and $\overleftarrow{\mathbf{h}}_i$ are sequences of vectors computed by a forward and a backward LSTM. an LSTM-cell is applied at each step to complete the following computations:

$$\begin{pmatrix} i_{i,t} \\ f_{i,t} \\ o_{i,t} \\ c_{i,t} \end{pmatrix} = \begin{pmatrix} \sigma \\ \sigma \\ \sigma \\ \tanh \end{pmatrix} U \begin{pmatrix} E^w x_{i,t} \\ h_{i,t-1} \end{pmatrix} \tag{1a}$$

$$\tilde{c}_{i,t} = f_{i,t} \odot \tilde{c}_{i,t-1} + i_{i,t} \odot c_{i,t} \tag{1b}$$

$$h_{i,t} = LSTM\text{-}cell(x_{i,t}, h_{i,t-1}) \tag{1c}$$

$$= o_{i,t} \odot \tanh(\tilde{c}_{i,t}) \tag{1d}$$

$i_{i,t}, f_{i,t}, o_{i,t}, c_{i,t}$ are the input, forget, output gates, and a contemporary central memory that control the information flow of the previous contexts and the current input. σ and $\tanh$ denotes element-wise sigmoid and tanh function. E^w is an embedding matrix that maps an input word $x_{i,t}$ to a x-dimensional vector. Each $h_{i,t}$ is a d-dimensional vector that can be viewed as the contextual representation of word $x_{i,t}$.

To obtain the sentence representation, we take a max pooling over the sentence, where for each dimension j of the vector $\hat{h}_i$, we have:

$$\hat{h}_i^j = \max_{t \in [1,...,T]} h_{i,t}^j, \; j = 1, ..., d. \tag{2}$$

The final classifier is defined as:

$$f^v(\mathbf{x}_i) = g(W\hat{h}_i + b), \tag{3}$$

where $g()$ is the softmax function, W and b are model parameters that are jointly learned with the BiLSTM parameters.

Generator. The generator for the ending valence-controlled story generation is a conditional language model, where the probability of generating each word is denoted as $p(w_t|w_1^{t-1}, l; \theta)$; l represents the ending valence label and θ represents model parameters. We learn valence embeddings for the ending valence labels to facilitate the computation. Formally, we learn an embedding matrix E^l to map each label l^k into a vector:

$$e_l^k = E^l[l^k],$$

where E^l is a $m \times p$ matrix that maps each label (p of them) into a m-dimensional vector. The ending valence embeddings dimension are made the same as the word embedding dimension for simplicity.

We add the ending valence as follows:

$$p(w_t|w_1^{t-1}, l; \theta) = \begin{cases} g(V\mathcal{F}(e_l, \mathcal{F}(w_{t-1}, h_{t-1}))), t = s \\ g(V\mathcal{F}(w_{t-1}, h_{t-1})), t = others \end{cases} \quad (4)$$

where s denotes the position right before the ending sentence, $g()$ is the softmax function, $\mathcal{F}$ means the computations of an LSTM-cell, and V denotes parameters that perform a linear transformation. We treat the ending valence as an additional input to the story. The valence embeddings are jointly learned with other model parameters.

2.2 Storyline Control

Li et al. (2013) introduced plot graphs which contain events and their relations to represent storyline. Although the representation is rich, these plot graphs are hard to define and curate without highly specialized knowledge. In this pilot study, we follow what Yan (2016) did for poetry, to use *a sequence of words* as the storyline. We further confine the words to appear in the original story.

Analyzer. The analyzer for storyline control is an *extractor* that extracts a sequence of words $\mathbf{k}_i = \{k_{i,1}, k_{i,2}, \ldots, k_{i,r}\}$ from each story $\mathbf{x}_i$. The k_is are ordered according to their order in the story. We adapt the RAKE algorithm (Rose et al., 2010) for keyword extraction, which builds document graphs and weights the importance of each word combining several word-level and graph-level criteria. We extract the most important word from each sentence as the storyline.

Generator. The generator for storyline-controlled generation is also a conditional language model. Specifically, we employ the seq2seq model with attention (Bahdanau et al., 2014) implemented in OpenNMT (Klein et al., 2017). Specifically, the storyline words are encoded into vectors by a BiLSTM: $\mathbf{h}^k = BiLSTM(\mathbf{k}) = [\overrightarrow{\mathbf{h}}^k; \overleftarrow{\mathbf{h}}^k]$, and the decoder generate each word according to the probability:

$$p(w_t|w_1^{t-1}, \mathbf{h}^k; \theta) = g(V^l s_t) \quad (5a)$$

$$s_t = \mathcal{F}^{att}(w_{t-1}, s_{t-1}, c_t) \quad (5b)$$

$$c_t = \sum_{j=1}^{r} \alpha_{tj} h_j^k \quad (5c)$$

$$\alpha_{tj} = \frac{\exp(a(s_{t-1}, h_j^k))}{\sum_{p=1}^{r} \exp(a(s_{t-1}, h_p^k))} \quad (5d)$$

Agreement experiment	Cases	Agreement
Researcher vs. Researcher	150	83%
Turkers vs. Researcher	150	78%
Classifier vs. Turkers	3980	69%
Always *happyEnding*	3980	58%

Table 1: Annotation agreement for labeling story ending valence. Labels are *happyEnding*, *sadEnding*, or *cannotTell*. The automatic classifier trained on 3980 turker annotated stories achieved much better results than the majority baseline on 5-fold cross-validation.

Method	PPL
uncontrolled model	24.63
Storyline controlled	**18.36**

Table 2: Perplexities on the ROCstories development data. When storylines are given, the controlled models achieve lower perplexity than the uncontrolled one.

$g()$ again denotes the softmax function, and V^l denotes parameters that perform a linear transformation. $\mathcal{F}^{att}()$ in Equation 5b denotes the computations of an LSTM-cell with attention mechanism, where the context vector c_t is computed by an weighted summation of the storyline words vectors as in Equation 5c, and the weights are computed from some alignment function $a()$ as in Equation 5d.

3 Experimental Setup

We conduct experiments on the ROCstories dataset (Mostafazadeh et al., 2016), which consists of 98,162 five-line stories for training, and 1871 stories each for the development and test sets. We treat the first four sentences of each story as the body and the last sentence as the ending. We build analyzers to annotate the ending valence and the storyline for every story, and train the two controlled generators with 98,162 annotated stories.

3.1 Ending Valence Annotation

We conduct a three-stage data collection procedure to gather ending valence annotations and train a classifier to analyze the whole corpora. We classify all the stories into *happyEnding*, *sadEnding*, or *cannotTell*. Table 1 summarizes the results.

In the first stage, two researchers annotate 150 stories to gauge the feasibility of the task. It is nontrivial, as the agreement between the two researchers is only 83%, mainly because of the *cannotTell* case[2]. The second stage collects larger-

---

[2]The inter-annotator agreement is 95% if we exclude the instances that at least one person chose *cannotTell*.

Methods	Ending Valence				Storyline			
	Faithfulness		Coherence		Faithfulness		Coherence	
	avg score	% win	avg score	% win	avg score	% win	avg score	% win
Retrieve Human	3.20	19.6	2.89	16.4	**3.47**	**42.4**	3.44	17.6
Uncontrolled	3.26	27.8	**3.54**	**41.8**	2.82	20.8	3.54	29.2
Controlled-Generated	**3.44**	**52.6**	3.37	**41.8**	3.08	36.8	**3.74**	**53.2**

Table 3: Human evaluation for the ending valence (left) and storyline (right) controlled generation. Scores range in [1,5]. Three stories (one from each method) are grouped together so that people can give comparative scores. Faithfulness survey asks people to rate whether the generated stories reflect the given control factors. Coherence asks people to rate the coherence of the stories without considering the control factors. % win measures how often the generated result by one method is rated higher than others, excluding the instances that tie on the highest score.

scale annotations from AMT. We gather 3980 annotated stories with the turker-researcher agreement at 78%. A classifier as described in Section 2.1 is then trained to analyze the whole ROCstories corpora. Using 5-fold cross-validation, we estimate the accuracy of the classifier to be 69%[3], which, while not terribly impressive, is an 11% improvement over the majority baseline (*happyEnding*). Considering the low inter-annotator agreement on this problem, we consider this a decent analyzer.

4 Experimental Results

We compare the controlled generation under our proposed framework with the uncontrolled generation. We design the experiments to answer the following research questions:

1. How does the controlled generation framework affect the generation quantitatively?

2. Does the proposed framework enables controls to the stories while maintaining the coherence of the stories?

To answer the former question, we design automatic evaluations that measure the perplexity of the models given appropriate and inappropriate controls. For the latter question, we design human evaluations to compare the generated stories from controlled and uncontrolled versions in terms of the document-level coherence and the faithfulness to the control factors.

4.1 Automatic Evaluation

The advantages of the automatic evaluation is that it can be conducted at scale and gives panoramic views of the systems. We compute the perplexities of different models on the ROCstories development dataset. Table 2 shows the results for

the storyline experiments. With the additional storyline information, it is easier for the generation model to guess what will happen next in a story, thus yield lower perplexities. We conduct the same experiments for ending valence controlled generation and observe the same. However, since ending valence is only one bit of information, the perplexity difference is only 0.8.

4.2 Human Evaluation

We conduct a human evaluation with 1000 story groups for each setting. Each group consists of stories from: (1) the uncontrolled LSTM generation model, (2) controlled generation with our framework, and (3) a contrastive method which retrieves and re-ranks existing sentences in the training data. Users are asked to rate the three stories on a 1-5 scale with respect to faithfulness (whether stories reflect the control factor), and coherence. All the evaluations are conducted on Amazon Mechanic Turk. We compute the average score and percentage win of each method. Table 3 summarizes the results.

Ending Valence For the ending valence control, we supply each system with the first 4 sentences from ROCStories test set and an ending valence randomly assigned by a human. The systems generate endings[4]. We only let the systems generate *happyEnding* or *sadEnding* stories, with the ratio around 1:1. Faithfulness is defined as whether the generated stories reflect the given ending valence.

The contrastive method retrieves existing happy or sad endings from the training data instead of generating new sentences. Specifically, we gather all the stories that are annotated with *happyEndings* from the 3980 annotated stories in one set, and all the *sadEndings* in another set. When the given ending valence is *happyEnding*, the sys-

---

[3]We included the *cannotTell* cases and conducted a 3-class classification.

[4]The uncontrolled LSTM generation model has no way to take the ending valence input.

Story Body	Setting	Ending
sarah had been dreaming of visiting europe for years. she had finally saved enough for the trip. she landed in spain and traveled east across the continent. she did n't like how different everything was.	Human	sarah decided she preferred home over europe.
	No-Valence-Control	sarah was so happy that she had a great time.
	Happy-Generated	sarah was happy to go home.
	Sad-Generated	sarah was very disappointed.
	Happy-Retrieved	they both had a lot of fun.
	Sad-Retrieved	I had to go to the hospital.
samuel loved reading old science fiction stories. he collected books by hg wells and jules verne. his favorite was hg wells. his father gave him a copy of the island of dr moreau.	Human	he loved it!
	No-Valence-Control	he was so happy to see the book.
	Happy-Generated	he was very happy to see the new book.
	Sad-Generated	he was so sad that he couldn't find his book.
	Happy-Retrieved	by the end of the day, he was glad he had gone!
	Sad-Retrieved	bob got very sick and had to go to the hospital.

Table 4: Samples of endings generated by given the first four sentences of a story and an ending valence. The uncontrolled version cannot take the designated ending valence into account, while both the controlled versions reflect the correct valence.

Users' Storyline	Generated Story
john angry meeting park happy	john was a very angry person. he was angry at his job. john decided to go to the park. john went to the park. john was very happy with his new job.
john angry meeting park wolf	john was very angry. he had a meeting at the park. he went to the park. he saw a wolf. john was very angry.
jennifer angry meeting park happy	jennifer was very angry. she had a meeting at the park. jennifer was not happy. she went to the park. jennifer was happy to be meeting her friend.
jennifer angry meeting park wolf scared	jennifer was very angry. she had a meeting at the park. she went to the park. she saw a wolf. jennifer was very angry.

Table 5: Samples of stories generated from user-given storyline words. The generated stories usually contains the words in the storyline. Changing one word in the storyline can result in another creative story.

tem scores all the sentences from the *happenEnding* set by combining it with the given 4 sentences, and using a trained uncontrolled generation model to compute the likelihood. This chooses the most coherent *happyEnding* for the given story. Similarly for the *sadEnding* stories. Table 3 shows that the proposed analyze-to-generate framework ("Controlled-Generated") achieves the highest faithfulness score while retaining similar coherence as the uncontrolled one.

Storyline For storyline control, we supply each system with 5 words as a storyline. The systems generate stories accordingly. Storyline words are extracted from the ROCstories test set. The uncontrolled generation model cannot take this input; it generates random stories. Faithfulness is defined as whether the generated stories follow the given storyline.

The contrastive method retrieves human written sentences in the training data to compose stories. Specifically, it follows the given storyline words order to retrieve sentences from the training data. The trained uncontrolled generation model scores each sentence based on existing previous sentences and choose the highest scoring sentence for each word in the storyline. If a word in the storyline has never appeared in the training data, we simply skip it.

As shown in Table 3, the contrastive method achieves the highest faithfulness, probably because it guarantees the words in the storyline appear in the stories while the other systems cannot. However, the coherence of the contrastive method is lowest, because it is constrained by the existing sentences in the training data. Although an uncontrolled generation model is employed to encourage document-level coherence, the available choices are restricted. Our method achieves the best coherence and higher faithfulness score than the uncontrolled version.

4.3 Generation Samples

Table 4 shows two examples of the ending valence controlled generation. The uncontrolled model "No-Valence-Control" can generate coherent endings; However, it cannot alter the ending valence. On the other hand, the two controlled models can generate different endings based on different ending valence. The contrastive retrieval method, restricted by the existing *happyEnding* and *sadEnding* in the training data, obtains endings that are not coherent with the whole story.

Table 5 demonstrates some examples from the storyline controlled generation. The storyline words are user supplied. We can see that this provides fun interactions: changing one word in the storyline can result in a creative new story.

5 Conclusion

We proposed an analyze-to-generate framework that enables controllable story generation. The framework is generally applicable for many control factors. In this paper, two instantiations of the framework are explored to control the ending valence and the storyline of stories. Experiments show that our framework enables human controls while achieving better coherence than an uncontrolled generation models. In the future, we will explore other control factors and better controllable generation models to adding the control factors into the generated stories. The current analyze-to-generate framework is done in a pipeline fashion. We also plan to explore the joint training of the analyzer and the generator to improve the quality of both.

Acknowledgements

We thank the anonymous reviewers for the useful comments and the suggestion for the right terminology of "ending valence". This work is supported by Contract W911NF-15-1-0543 with the US Defense Advanced Research Projects Agency (DARPA).

References

Dzmitry Bahdanau, Kyunghyun Cho, and Yoshua Bengio. 2014. Neural machine translation by jointly learning to align and translate. *arXiv preprint arXiv:1409.0473* .

Selmer Bringsjord and David Ferrucci. 1999. *Artificial intelligence and literary creativity: Inside the mind of brutus, a storytelling machine.* Psychology Press.

Marc Cavazza, David Pizzi, Fred Charles, Thurid Vogt, and Elisabeth André. 2009. Emotional input for character-based interactive storytelling. In *Proceedings of The 8th International Conference on Autonomous Agents and Multiagent Systems-Volume 1*. International Foundation for Autonomous Agents and Multiagent Systems, pages 313–320.

Xi Chen, Yan Duan, Rein Houthooft, John Schulman, Ilya Sutskever, and Pieter Abbeel. 2016. Infogan: Interpretable representation learning by information maximizing generative adversarial nets. In *Proceedings of Advances in Neural Information Processing Systems*.

Giovanna Egidi and Richard J Gerrig. 2009. How valence affects language processing: Negativity bias and mood congruence in narrative comprehension. *Memory & cognition* 37(5):547–555.

Jessica Ficler and Yoav Goldberg. 2017. Controlling linguistic style aspects in neural language generation. In *Proceedings of the Workshop on Stylistic Variation*. pages 94–104.

Zhenxin Fu, Xiaoye Tan, Nanyun Peng, Dongyan Zhao, and Rui Yan. 2017. Style transfer in text: Exploration and evaluation. In *Proceedings of The 32nd AAAI Conference on Artificial Intelligence*.

Pablo Gervas, Belen Diaz-Agudo, Federico Peinado, and Raquel Hervas. 2005. Story plot generation based on CBR. *Knowledge-Based Systems* 18(4):235–242.

Marjan Ghazvininejad, Xing Shi, Jay Priyadarshi, and Kevin Knight. 2017. Hafez: an interactive poetry generation system. *Proceedings of 55th Annual Meeting of the Association for Computational Linguistics, System Demonstrations* pages 43–48.

Sepp Hochreiter and Jurgen Schmidhuber. 1997. Long short-term memory. *Neural computation* 9(8):1735–1780.

Zhiting Hu, Zichao Yang, Xiaodan Liang, Ruslan Salakhutdinov, and Eric P Xing. 2017. Toward controlled generation of text. In *Proceedings of the International Conference on Machine Learning*. pages 1587–1596.

Ryan Kiros, Yukun Zhu, Ruslan Salakhutdinov, Richard Zemel, Raquel Urtasun, Antonio Torralba, and Sanja Fidler. 2015. Skip-thought vectors. In *Proceedings of Advances in neural information processing systems*.

Guillaume Klein, Yoon Kim, Yuntian Deng, Jean Senellart, and Alexander M. Rush. 2017. OpenNMT: Open-source toolkit for neural machine translation. In *ACL*.

Guillaume Lample, Neil Zeghidour, Nicolas Usunier, Antoine Bordes, Ludovic Denoyer, and Marc'Aurelio Ranzato. 2017. Fader networks: Manipulating images by sliding attributes. In *Proceedings of 31st Conference on Neural Information Processing Systems*.

Michael Lebowitz. 1987. Planning stories. In *Proceedings of the cognitive science society, Hillsdale*.

Boyang Li, Stephen Lee-Urban, George Johnston, and Mark Riedl. 2013. Story generation with crowd-sourced plot graphs. In *Proceedings of The 28th AAAI Conference on Artificial Intelligence*.

Lara Martin, Prithviraj Ammanabrolu, William Hancock, Shruti Singh, Brent Harrison, and Mark Riedl. 2017. Event representations for automated story generation with deep neural nets. In *Proceedings of the Thirty-Second AAAI Conference on Artificial Intelligence*.

James Meehan. 1977. TALE-SPIN, an interactive program that writes stories. In *Proceedings of The International Joint Conferences on Artificial Intelligence Organization*.

Nasrin Mostafazadeh, Nathanael Chambers, Xiaodong He, Devi Parikh, Dhruv Batra, Lucy Vanderwende, Pushmeet Kohli, and James Allen. 2016. A corpus and cloze evaluation for deeper understanding of commonsense stories. In *Proceedings of the Conference of the North American Chapter of the Association for Computational Linguistics: Human Language Technologies*.

Rafael Perez and Mike Sharples. 2001. MEXICA: A computer model of a cognitive account of creative writing. *Journal of Experimental & Theoretical Artificial Intelligence* 13(2):119–139.

Mark Riedl and Robert Young. 2010. Narrative planning: Balancing plot and character. *Journal of Artificial Intelligence Research* 39:217–268.

Melissa Roemmele, Sosuke Kobayashi, Naoya Inoue, and Andrew M Gordon. 2017. An RNN-based binary classifier for the story cloze test. *LSDSem 2017* page 74.

Stuart Rose, Dave Engel, Nick Cramer, and Wendy Cowley. 2010. Automatic keyword extraction from individual documents. *Text Mining: Applications and Theory* pages 1–20.

Tianxiao Shen, Tao Lei, Regina Barzilay, and Tommi Jaakkola. 2017. Style transfer from non-parallel text by cross-alignment. In *Proceedings of Advances in neural information processing systems*.

N Siddharth, Brooks Paige, Van de Meent, Alban Desmaison, Frank Wood, Noah D Goodman, Pushmeet Kohli, Philip HS Torr, et al. 2017. Learning disentangled representations with semi-supervised deep generative models. In *Proceedings of Advances in Neural Information Processing Systems*.

Ilya Sutskever, Oriol Vinyals, and Quoc Le. 2014. Sequence to sequence learning with neural networks. In *Proceedings of Advances in neural information processing systems*.

Reid Swanson and Andrew Gordon. 2012. Say anything: Using textual case-based reasoning to enable open-domain interactive storytelling. *ACM Transactions on Interactive Intelligent Systems* 2(3):16.

Duyu Tang, Bing Qin, and Ting Liu. 2015. Document modeling with gated recurrent neural network for sentiment classification. In *Proceedings of the Conference on Empirical Methods in Natural Language Processing*. pages 1422–1432.

Scott R. Turner. 1993. *Minstrel: A Computer Model of Creativity and Storytelling*. Ph.D. thesis, Los Angeles, CA, USA. UMI Order no. GAX93-19933.

Di Wang, Nebojsa Jojic, Chris Brockett, and Eric Nyberg. 2017. Steering output style and topic in neural response generation. In *Proceedings of the Conference on Empirical Methods in Natural Language Processing*. pages 2130–2140.

Rui Yan. 2016. i, poet: Automatic poetry composition through recurrent neural networks with iterative polishing schema. In *Proceedings of The International Joint Conferences on Artificial Intelligence Organization*. pages 2238–2244.

An Encoder-decoder Approach to Predicting Causal Relations in Stories

Melissa Roemmele and Andrew S. Gordon
Institute for Creative Technologies, University of Southern California
roemmele@ict.usc.edu, gordon@ict.usc.edu

Abstract

We address the task of predicting causally related events in stories according to a standard evaluation framework, the Choice of Plausible Alternatives (COPA). We present a neural encoder-decoder model that learns to predict relations between adjacent sequences in stories as a means of modeling causality. We explore this approach using different methods for extracting and representing sequence pairs as well as different model architectures. We also compare the impact of different training datasets on our model. In particular, we demonstrate the usefulness of a corpus not previously applied to COPA, the ROCStories corpus. While not state-of-the-art, our results establish a new reference point for systems evaluated on COPA, and one that is particularly informative for future neural-based approaches.

1 Introduction

Automated story understanding is a long-pursued task in AI research (Dehn, 1981; Lebowitz, 1985; Meehan, 1977). It has been examined as a commonsense reasoning task, by which systems make inferences about events that prototypically occur in common experiences (e.g. going to a restaurant) (Schank and Abelson, 1977). Early work often failed to scale beyond narrow domains of stories due to the difficulty of automatically inducing story knowledge. The shift to data-driven AI established new opportunities to acquire this knowledge automatically from story corpora. The field of NLP now recognizes that the type of commonsense reasoning used to predict what happens next in a story, for example, is as important for natural language understanding systems as linguistic knowledge itself.

A barrier to this research has been the lack of standard evaluation schemes for benchmarking progress. The Story Cloze Test (Mostafazadeh

et al., 2016) was recently developed to address this, with a focus on predicting events that are temporally and causally related within common real-world scenarios. The Story Cloze Test involves selecting which of two given sentences best completes a particular story. Related to this is the Choice of Plausible Alternatives (COPA) task (Roemmele et al., 2011), which uses the same binary-choice format to elicit a prediction for either the cause or effect of a given story event. While the Story Cloze Test involves predicting the ending of a story, COPA items focus specifically on commonsense knowledge related to identifying causal relations between sequences.

The competitive approaches to narrative prediction evaluated by the Story Cloze Test largely involve neural networks trained to distinguish between correct and incorrect endings of stories (Cai et al., 2017, e.g.). A neural network approach has yet to be applied to the related COPA task. In the current paper, we initiate this investigation into these models for COPA. In particular, we evaluate an encoder-decoder model that predicts the probability that a particular sequence follows another in a story. Our experiments explore a few different variables for configuring this approach. First, we examine how to extract temporally related sequence pairs provided as input to the model. Second, we vary the use of feed-forward versus recurrent layers within the model. Third, we assess different vector-based representations of the sequence pairs. Finally, we compare our model using different narrative corpora for training, including the ROCStories corpus which was developed in conjunction with the Story Cloze Test. Our results are presented in comparison to existing systems applied to COPA, which involve lexical co-occurrence statistics gathered from web corpora. Our best-performing model achieves an accuracy of 66.2% on the COPA test set, which falls short of

50

Proceedings of the First Workshop on Storytelling, pages 50–59
New Orleans, Louisiana, June 5, 2018. ©2018 Association for Computational Linguistics

the current state-of-the-art of 71.2% (Sasaki et al., 2017). Interestingly, this best result utilizes the ROCStories for training, which is only a small fraction of the size of the datasets used in existing approaches. Applying our model to these larger datasets actually yields significantly worse performance, suggesting that the model is sensitive to the density of commonsense knowledge contained in its training set. We conclude that this density is far more influential to COPA performance than just data quantity, and further success on the task will depend on methods for isolating implicit commonsense knowledge in text.

2 Choice of Plausible Alternatives

The Choice of Plausible Alternatives (COPA) is composed of 1,000 items, where each item contains three sentences, a *premise* and two *alternatives*, as well as a prompt specifying the relation between them. The items are divided equally into development and test sets of 500 items each. The goal is to select which alternative conveys the more plausible cause (or effect, based on the prompt) of the premise sentence. Half of the prompts elicit the more plausible effect of the premise event, while the other half ask for the more plausible cause of the premise.

1. **Premise:** The homeowners disliked their nosy neighbors. *What happened as a result?*
   Alternative 1:* They built a fence around their property.
   Alternative 2: They hosted a barbecue in their backyard.

2. **Premise:** The man fell unconscious. *What was the cause of this?*
   Alternative 1:* The assailant struck the man in the head.
   Alternative 2: The assailant took the man's wallet.

Above are examples of COPA items, where the designated correct alternative for each is starred. In a given item, both alternatives refer to events that could be found within the same story, but the correct one conveys a more coherent causal relation. All sentences consist of a single clause with a past tense verb. COPA items were written by a single author and then validated by other annotators to ensure human accuracy approximated 100%. See Roemmele et al. (2011) for further details about the authoring and validation process.

3 Existing Approaches

Roemmele et al. (2011) presented a baseline approach to COPA that focused on lexical co-occurrence statistics gathered from story corpora. The general idea is that a causal relation between two story events can be modeled by the proximity of the words that express the events. This approach uses the Pointwise Mutual Information (PMI) statistic (Church and Hanks, 1990) to compute the number of times two words co-occur within the same context (i.e. within a certain N number of words of each other in a story) relative to their overall frequency. This co-occurence measure is order-sensitive such that the first word in the pair is designated as the cause word and the second as the effect word, based on the assumption that cause events are more often described before their effects in stories, relative to the reverse. To calculate an overall causality score for two sequences $S1$ and $S2$, each cause word c in $S1$ is paired with each effect word e in $S2$, and the PMI scores of all word pairs are averaged: $\frac{\sum_{c \in S1} \sum_{e \in S2} PMI(c,e)}{|S1| * |S2|}$. For a given COPA item, the predicted alternative is the one that has the higher causality score with regard to the premise. Since the scores are asymmetric in assuming $S1$ is the cause of $S2$, COPA items that elicit the more plausible effect (i.e. items where "What happened as a result?" is the prompt) assign the premise and alternative to $S1$ and $S2$ respectively, whereas this assignment is reversed for items where "What was the cause of this?" is the prompt. Gordon et al. (2011) applied this approach to PMI scores taken from a corpus of one million stories extracted from personal weblogs, which were largely non-fiction stories about daily life events written from the first-person perspective. A co-occurrence between two words was counted when they appeared within 25 words of one another in the same story. This resulted in 65.2% accuracy on the COPA test set.

The PMI approach assumes a causal relation between events can be captured to some degree by their temporal co-occurrence in a story. Luo et al. (2016) introduced a variation that alternatively focuses on explicit mentions of causality in text, referred to as the CausalNet approach. They extracted sequences matching lexical templates that signify causality, e.g. $S1$ LEADS TO $S2$, $S2$ RESULTS FROM $S1$, $S2$ DUE TO $S1$, where again $S1$ is the cause event and $S2$ is the effect. As before, a co-occurrence is counted between each pair of words (c, e) in $S1$ and $S2$, respectively. They propose a measure of *causal strength* that adapts the PMI statistic to model both necessary causality and sufficient causality for a given pair (c, e). In the measure for necessary causality, a discounting factor is applied to the overall frequency of c in the PMI statistic, which models the degree to which c must appear in order for e to appear. Alternatively, the measure for sufficient causality applies the discounting factor to the overall frequency of e, modeling the degree to which c alone will result in the occurrence of e. The necessary and sufficient PMI scores for a given word pair are combined into a single causal strength score. Akin to the previous approach, the overall causality score for two sequences is given by averaging the scores for their word pairs. See Luo et al. for further technical details about the causal strength measure.

Luo et al. applied this approach to extract causal pairs from a corpus of approximately 1.6 billion web pages. They achieved 70.2% accuracy on the COPA test set, significantly outperforming the result from Gordon et al. (2011). Sasaki et al. (2017) evaluated the same CausalNet approach on a smaller corpus of web documents, ClueWeb[1], which contains 700 million pages. They discovered that treating multi-word phrases as discrete words in the pairs boosted accuracy to 71.2%. Both results indicate that causal knowledge can be extracted from large web data as an alternative to story corpora. Rather than assuming that causality is implicitly conveyed by temporally related sequences, they relied on explicit mentions of causality to filter data relevant to COPA. Still, a lot of causal knowledge in stories is not highlighted by specific lexical items. Consider the sequence "John starts a pot of coffee because he is sleepy", for example. This sequence would be extracted by the CausalNet approach since it contains one of the designated lexical markers of causality ("because"). However, the sequence "John is sleepy. He starts a pot of coffee" expresses the same causal relation but would not be captured, and we know by people's ability to answer COPA questions that they can infer this relation. Using a large web corpus can possibly compensate for missing these instances, since the same causal relations may be conveyed by sequences that contain explicit mentions of causality. However, it still means that a lot of causal information

is potentially being overlooked.

4 Neural Network Approach

As mentioned in the introduction, our work initiates the exploration of neural approaches to COPA. We focus here on an encoder-decoder architecture. Originally applied to machine translation (Cho et al., 2014), encoder-decoder models have been extended to other sequence modeling tasks like dialogue generation (Serban et al., 2016; Shang et al., 2015) and poetry generation (Ghazvininejad et al., 2016; Wang et al., 2016). We propose that this technique could be similarly useful for our task in establishing a mapping between cause-effect sequence pairs. This direct modeling of co-occurrence between sequences is unique from the previous work, which relies on co-occurrence between pairs of individual words.

4.1 Sequence Segmentation

The inputs and outputs for the encoder-decoder model are each word sequences. Given a corpus of stories as the training set for a model, we first segmented each story by clausal boundaries. This was done heuristically by analyzing the dependency parse of each sentence. Words whose dependency label was an adverbial clause modifier (ADVCL; e.g. "After I got home, I *got* a text from her."), conjunct (CONJ; "I dropped the glass and the glass *broke*."), or prepositional complement (PCOMP; "He took me to the hospital to *seek* treatment.") were detected as the heads of clauses distinct from the main clause. All contiguous words dependent on the same head word were segmented as a separate clause. These particular labels do not capture all clausal boundaries (for example, relative clauses are not detected), but they are intended to distinguish sequences that may refer to separate narrative events (e.g. "I dropped the glass" is segmented from "and the glass broke"). This is somewhat analogous to the segmentation performed by Luo et al. (2016) that splits cause and effect clauses according to lexical templates. The difference is that the parsing labels we use for segmentation do not explicitly indicate boundaries between causally related events. We did not perform an intrinsic evaluation of this procedure in terms of how often it correctly segmented narrative events. Instead, we evaluated its impact on COPA prediction by comparing it to traditional segmentation based on sentence boundaries for the

[1]lemurproject.org/clueweb12/

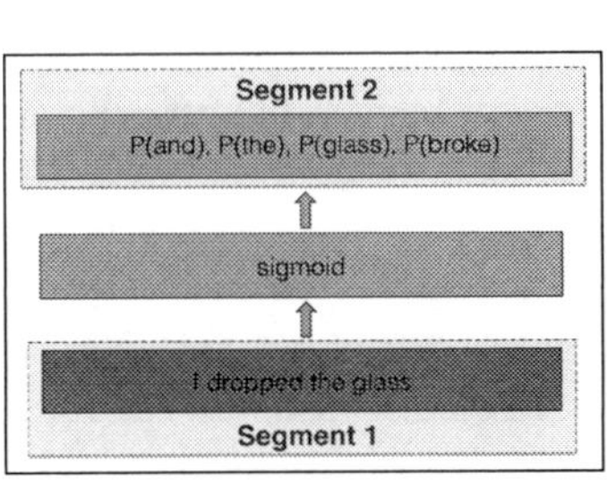

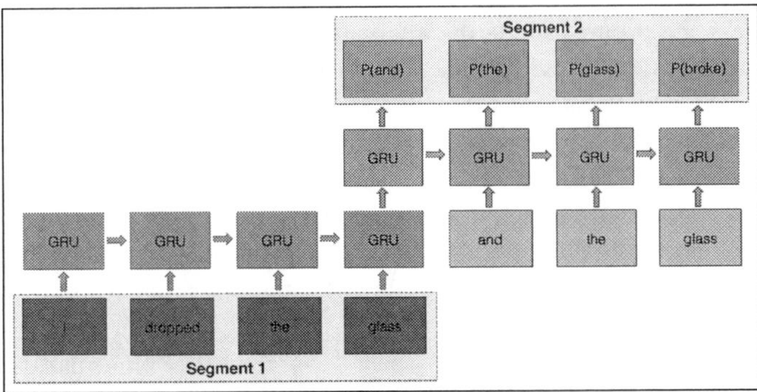

Figure 1: FFN (left) and RNN (right) encoder-decoder models

same model, as conveyed in Section 5.3.

4.2 Sequence Pairs

After segmenting the stories, we joined neighboring segments (i.e. clauses or sentences) into input-output segment pairs ($S1$, $S2$). In all of our experiments, we filtered pairs where one or both of the segments contained more than 20 words. We manipulated the temporal window within which these pairs were joined, by pairing all segments within N segments of each other. For a given segment at position t in a story, pairs were established between all segments in $segment_t, \ldots, segment_{t+N}$. For example, when N=1, a pair was formed with the next segment only ($segment_t, segment_{t+1}$); when N=2, pairs were formed between ($segment_t, segment_{t+1}$) and ($segment_t, segment_{t+2}$). By doing this, we intended to examine the proximity of causal information in a story according to its impact on COPA prediction; we expected that more adjacent clauses would contain stronger causal relations than more distant clauses. Gordon et al. (2011) analogously evaluated this by varying the number of words within which PMI pairs were formed, but without regard to sentence or clause boundaries.

4.3 Encoder-decoder Models

We examined two types of encoder-decoder models: one with feed-forward (FFN) layers and one with recurrent (RNN) layers (i.e. a sequence-to-sequence model), both shown in Figure 1. In both cases, the model implicitly assumes that the input segment $S1$ represents the cause of the output segment $S2$, so the model learns to predict that $S2$ will appear as the effect of $S1$. The theoretical motivation for comparing the FFN and RNN is to determine the importance of word order for this task.

The existing COPA approaches only accounted for word order to the extent of capturing word pairs within the same context of N words (though Sasaki et al. (2017) also accounted for multi-word expressions). The FFN encoder-decoder ignores word order. The model is very simple: both the input and output segments are collapsed into flat n-dimensional vectors of word counts (i.e. bag-of-words), so the hidden (encoder) layer observes all words in each segment in parallel. On the output (decoder) layer (which has sigmoid activation like the encoder), the FFN computes a score for each word indicating its probability of appearing anywhere in output segment.

In contrast, the RNN captures word order in the segments. In particular, it uses a recurrent (encoder) layer with Gated Recurrent Units (GRUs) (Cho et al., 2014) to iteratively encode the input sequence, and another recurrent (decoder) layer to represent output segment. The final hidden state of the encoder layer after observing the whole input is provided as the initial hidden state to the decoder. The decoder then iteratively computes a representation of the output sequence that is conditioned upon the input segment. For each timepoint in this decoder layer, a softmax layer is applied to predict a probability distribution over each word being observed in the segment at that particular timepoint. Both the FFN and RNN encoder-decoders are trained using the cross-entropy loss function to maximize the output word probabilities observed during training.

Once trained, a model predicts the likelihood that a cause sequence $S1$ given as input results in an effect sequence $S2$ based on the mean probability of the words in $S2$ computed by the model. When applied to COPA, consistent with the methodology described in Section 3, in items where the prompt elicits the alternative that conveys the effect of the premise, the premise is designated as $S1$ and the alternative as $S2$. In contrast, when the item elicits the alternative describing the most likely cause of the premise, an alternative is assigned to $S1$ and the premise to $S2$. In considering the two alternatives in a COPA item, the one contained in the $(S1, S2)$ pair that obtains the highest score is predicted as more plausible.

5 Initial Experiments

5.1 ROCStories Corpus

The PMI and CausalNet approaches to COPA made use of large web corpora. Gordon et al. (2011) proposed that stories are a rich source for the commonsense knowledge needed to answer COPA questions. Mostafazadeh et al. (2016) followed this proposal by releasing the ROCStories corpus[2], intended to be applied to commonsense reasoning tasks. The ROCStories corpus has yet to be utilized for COPA prediction. This dataset consists of 97,027 five-sentence narratives authored via crowdsourcing. In contrast to weblog stories, these stories were written with the specific objective to minimize discourse complexity and explicate prototypical causal and temporal relations between events in salient everyday scenarios. COPA items also target these latent commonsense relations, so the ROCStories appear to be particularly suitable for this domain. Table 1 shows some examples of stories in this corpus and corresponding COPA items that address the same causal knowledge. The ROCStories corpus is dramatically smaller than the datasets used in the work described in Section 3.

5.2 Procedure

We applied the methodology outlined in Section 4 to pairs of sequences from the ROCStories corpus. Our first set of experiments varied segmentation (clause versus sentence boundaries), distance between segments (N=1 to N=4), and the type of encoder-decoder (FFN or RNN). Note that N=4 is the maximum setting when using sentence boundaries since there are five sentences in each story, so here pairs will be formed between all sentences. For all experiments, we filtered grammatical words (i.e. all words except for adjectives, adverbs, nouns, and verbs) and lemmatized all segments, consistent with Luo et al. (2016). COPA

---

[2]cs.rochester.edu/nlp/rocstories/

items intentionally do not contain proper nouns, so we excluded them as well. We assembled a model lexicon that included each word occurring at least five times in the data, which totaled 9,299 words in the ROCStories. All other words were mapped to a generic <UNKNOWN> token.

The hidden layers of the FFN and RNN models each consisted of 500 dimensions. The RNN had an additional word embedding layer of 300 nodes in order to transform discrete word indices in the input segments into distributed vectors. They were both trained for 50 epochs using the Adam optimizer (Kingma and Ba, 2015) with a batch size of 100 pairs. After each epoch, we evaluated the model on the COPA development set and saved the weights that obtained the highest accuracy.

5.3 Results

Table 2 shows the results of these different configurations in terms of COPA accuracy. We include the results on the development set as a reference because they tended to vary from the test results. Most notably, the FFN outperformed the RNN universally, suggesting that the order of words in the segments did not provide a strong signal for prediction beyond the presence of the words themselves. Among the FFN results, the model trained on clauses with N=4 obtained the highest accuracy on the development set (66.0%), and was tied for the highest test accuracy with the model trained on clauses with N=3 (66.2%). The model with N=4 was trained on three times as many pairs as the model with N=1. We can conclude that some of these additional pairs pertained to causality, despite not appearing adjacently in the story. The impact of clause versus sentence segmentation is less clear from these results, given that the best result of 66.2% accuracy using clauses is only trivially better than the corresponding result for sentences (66.0% for N=4).

5.4 Other Findings

5.4.1 Alternative Input Representations

In the FFN model evaluated above, the input segments were simply represented as bag-of-words vectors indicating the count of each word in the segment. Alternatively, we explored the use of pretrained word embeddings to represent the segments. We proposed that because they provide the model with some initial signal about lexical relations, the embeddings could facilitate more

ROCStories Instance	COPA Item
Susie went away to Nantucket. She wanted to relax. When she got there it was amazing. The waves were so relaxing. Susie never wanted to leave.	**Premise:** The man went away for the weekend. What was the cause of this? **Alt 1*:** He wanted to relax. **Alt 2:** He felt content.
Albert wanted to enter the spelling bee, but he was a bad speller. He practiced every day for the upcoming contest. When Albert felt that he was ready, he entered the spelling bee. In the very last round, Albert failed when he misspelled a word. Albert was very proud of himself for winning the second place trophy.	**Premise:** The girl received a trophy. What was the cause of this? **Alt 1*:** She won a spelling bee. **Alt 2:** She made a new friend.
Anna was lonely. One day, Anna went to the grocery store. Outside the store, she met a woman who was giving away kittens. Anna decided to adopt one of those kittens. Anna no longer felt lonely with her new pet.	**Premise:** The woman felt lonely. What happened as a result? **Alt 1:** She renovated her kitchen. **Alt 2*:** She adopted a cat.
April is fascinated by health and medicine. She decided to become a doctor. She studied very hard in college and medical school. April graduated at the top of her medical school class. April now works in a hospital as a doctor.	**Premise:** The woman wanted to be a doctor. What happened as a result? **Alt 1:** She visited the hospital. **Alt 2*:** She went to medical school.

Table 1: Examples of stories in ROCStories corpus and similar COPA items

Segment	N	# Pairs	FFN		RNN	
			Dev	Test	Dev	Test
Sentence	1	389,680	64.8	64.4	63.4	54.4
	2	682,334	65.2	65.4	61.2	57.6
	3	877,963	63.8	63.8	60.2	55.4
	4	976,568	63.8	66.0	59.4	55.6
Clause	1	539,342	64.2	63.6	59.4	56.8
	2	981,677	65.2	65.0	59.2	54.6
	3	1,327,010	65.4	**66.2**	63.4	58.0
	4	1,575,340	66.0	**66.2**	61.2	56.6

Table 2: Accuracy by segmentation unit and pair distance (N) for the FFN and RNN encoder-decoders trained on ROCStories

Model	Dev	Test
FFN (above)	66.0	**66.2**
FFN GloVe	65.0	61.6
FFN ConceptNet	61.6	62.4
FFN Skip-thought	66.8	63.8

Table 3: Accuracy of FFN trained on ROCStories with different input representations

specifically learning causal relations. We experimented with three sets of embedding representations. First, we encoded the words in each input segment as the sum of their GloVe embeddings[3] (Pennington et al., 2014), which represent words according to a global log-bilinear regression model trained on word co-occurrence counts in the Common Crawl corpus. We also did this using ConceptNet embeddings[4] (Li et al., 2013), which apply the word2vec skip-gram model (Mikolov et al., 2013) to tuples that specifically define commonsense knowledge relations (e.g. soak in hotspring CAUSES get pruny skin). Lastly, we used skip-thought vectors[5] (Kiros et al., 2015), which compute one embedding representation for an entire sentence, and thus represent the sentence beyond just the sum of its individual words. Analogous to how word embedding models are trained to predict words near a given target word in a text, the skip-thought vectors represent sentences according to their relation to adjacent sentences, such that sentences with similar meanings are expected to have similar vectors. The provided skip-thought vectors are trained on the BookCorpus dataset, which is described in Section 6.

We trained the FFN model on the ROCStories with each of these three sets of embeddings. Because they obtained the best performance in the previous experiments, we configured the models to use clause segmentation and distance N=4 in constructing the pairs. Table 3 shows the results of these models, compared alongside the best result from above with the standard bag-of-words representation. Neither the GloVe nor ConceptNet embeddings performed better than the bag-of-words vectors (61.6% and 62.4% test accuracy, respectively). The skip-thought vectors performed better than bag-of-words representation on the development set (66.8%), but this improvement did not

[3]nlp.stanford.edu/projects/glove/

[4]ttic.uchicago.edu/ kgimpel/commonsense.html

[5]github.com/ryankiros/skip-thoughts

scale to the test set (63.8%).

5.4.2 Phrases

Model	Dev	Test
FFN (above)	66.0	**66.2**
FFN Phrases	62.6	64.8

Table 4: Accuracy of FFN trained on ROCStories with explicit phrase representations

As mentioned above, Sasaki et al. (2017) found that modeling multi-word phrases as individual words was helpful for the CausalNet approach. The RNN encoder-decoder has the opportunity to recognize phrases by modeling sequential dependencies between words, but Table 2 indicated this model was not successful relative to the FFN model. To assess whether the FFN model would benefit from phrase information, we merged all phrases in the training corpus into individual word tokens in the same manner as Sasaki et al., using their same list of phrases. We again filtered all tokens that occurred fewer than five times in the data, which resulted in the vocabulary increasing from 9,299 words to 10,694 when the phrases were included. We trained the same FFN model in Table 2 that achieved the best result (clause segmentation, N=4, and bag-of-words input representation). The test accuracy, relayed for clarity in Table 4 alongside the above best result, was 64.8%, indicating there was no benefit to modeling phrases in this particular configuration.

5.4.3 Comparison with Existing Approaches

Model	Dev	Test
FFN (above)	66.0	**66.2**
PMI	60.0	62.4
CausalNet	50.2	51.8

Table 5: Accuracy of PMI and CausalNet trained on ROCStories

To establish a comparison between our encoder-decoder approach and the existing models applied to the same dataset, we trained the PMI model on the ROCStories. Rather than using a fixed word window, we computed the PMI scores for all words in each story, which generally corresponds to using distance N=4 among sentence segments in the encoder-decoder. Table 5 shows that this approach had 62.4% test accuracy, so our new approach outperformed it on this particular dataset.

For completeness, we also applied the CausalNet approach to this dataset. Its poor performance (51.8%) is unsurprising, because the lexical templates used to extract causal pairs only matched 4,964 sequences in the ROCStories. This demonstrates that most of the causal information contained in these stories is conveyed implicitly.

6 Experiments on Other Datasets

Gordon et al. (2011) found that the PMI approach trained on blog stories performed better on COPA than the same model trained on books in Project Gutenburg[6], despite the much larger size of the latter. Beyond this, there has been limited exploration of the impact of different training datasets on COPA prediction, so we were motivated to examine this. Thus, we applied the FFN encoder-decoder approach to the following datasets:

Visual Storytelling (VIST): 50,200 five-sentence stories[7] authored through crowdsourcing in support of research on vision-to-language tasks (Huang et al., 2016). Participants were prompted to write a story from a sequence of photographs depicting salient "storyable" events.

CNN/DailyMail corpus: 312,085 bullet-item summaries[8] of news articles, which have been used for work on reading comprehension and summarization (Chen et al., 2016; See et al., 2017).

CMU Book/Movie Plot Summaries (CMU Plots): 58,862 plot summaries[9] from Wikipedia, which have been used for story modeling tasks like inferring relations between story characters (Bamman et al., 2014; Srivastava et al., 2016).

BookCorpus: 8,032 self-published fiction novels, a subset of the full corpus[10] of 11,000 books.

Blog Stories: 1 million weblog stories used in the COPA experiments by Gordon et al. (2011) identified above.

ClueWeb Pairs: Approximately 150 million sequence pairs extracted from the ClueWeb corpus by Sasaki et al. (2017) using the CausalNet lexical templates method.

6.1 Procedure and Results

We trained the FFN model with the best-performing configuration from the ROCStories ex-

---

[6]gutenberg.org/
[7]visionandlanguage.net/VIST/
[8]github.com/danqi/rc-cnn-dailymail
[9]cs.cmu.edu/~ark/personas/;
cs.cmu.edu/~dbamman/booksummaries.html
[10]yknzhu.wixsite.com/mbweb

Dataset	# Pairs	Dev	Test
ROCStories-Half	762,130	64.0	62.6
VIST	854,810	58.2	49.2
ROCStories-Full	1,575,340	66.0	**66.2**
CNN/DailyMail	3,255,010	59.4	51.8
CMU Plots	6,094,619	57.8	51.0
ClueWeb Pairs	157,426,812	60.8	61.2
Blog Stories	222,564,571	58.4	57.2
BookCorpus	310,001,015	58.2	55.0

Table 6: Accuracy of the FFN encoder-decoder on different datasets

periments (clause segments, N=4, bag-of-words input). After determining that the lexicon used in the previous experiments included most of the words (93.5%) in the COPA development set, we re-used this same lexicon to avoid the inefficiency of assembling a new one for each separate corpus. We also trained a model on the initial 45,502 stories in the ROCStories (ROCStories-Half) to further analyze the impact of this dataset.

Table 6 shows the results for these datasets compared alongside the ROCStories result from above (ROCStories-Full), listed in ascending order of the number of training pairs they contain. As shown, none of the other datasets reach the level of accuracy of ROCStories-Full (66.2%). Even the model trained on only the initial half of this corpus outperforms the others (62.6%). The next closest result is for the ClueWeb Pairs, which had 61.2% test accuracy despite containing 100 times more pairs than the ROCStories. The larger Blog Stories and BookCorpus datasets did not have much impact, despite that the Blog Stories obtained 65.2% accuracy in the PMI approach. One speculative explanation for this is that our approach is highly dependent on the *density* of COPA-relevant knowledge contained in a dataset. As mentioned above, authors of the ROCStories were instructed to emphasize the most obvious possibilities for 'what happens next' in prototypical scenarios. These expectations align with the correct COPA alternatives. However, naturally occurring stories often focus on events that violate commonsense expectations, since these events make for more salient stories (Schank and Ableson, 1995). Thus, they may show greater diversity in 'what happens next' relative to the ROCStories. This diversity was seemingly more distracting for our encoder-decoder architecture than for the existing approaches. Accordingly, despite all being related to narrative, the VIST, CNN/DailyMail, and CMU Plots datasets were also ineffective on the test set with regard to this model.

7 Conclusion

In summary, we pursued a neural encoder-decoder approach for predicting causally related events in the COPA framework. To our knowledge this is the first work to evaluate a neural-based model for this task. Our best result obtained 66.2% accuracy. This is lower than the current state-of-the-art of 71.2%, but our experiments motivate some opportunities for future work. We demonstrated the usefulness of the ROCStories for this task, as our model appeared to benefit from its density of commonsense knowledge. The gap between 66.2% and 71.2% is not dramatic in light of the massive size advantage of the data used to obtain the latter result. However, the ROCStories corpus is a crowdsourced dataset and thus will not grow naturally over time like web data, so it may not be practical to rely exclusively on this type of specially authored resource either. The CausalNet approach proposed a useful way to isolate commonsense knowledge in generic text by relying on causal cues, but because many causal relations are not marked by specific lexical items, it still overlooks a lot that is relevant to COPA. On the other hand, not all temporally related events in a story are causally related. Because we did not make this distinction, some of the pairs we modeled were likely not indicative of causality and thus may not have contributed accurately to COPA prediction. Research on automatically detecting more latent linguistic features specifically associated with the expression of causal knowledge in text would likely have a large impact on this endeavor.

Acknowledgments

We would like to thank the authors of Sasaki et al. (2017) for sharing the data and resources associated with their work.

The projects or efforts depicted were or are sponsored by the U.S. Army. The content or information presented does not necessarily reflect the position or the policy of the Government, and no official endorsement should be inferred.

References

David Bamman, Brendan O'Connor, and Noah A Smith. 2014. Learning latent personas of film characters. In *Proceedings of the Annual Meeting of the Association for Computational Linguistics (ACL)*. page 352.

Zheng Cai, Lifu Tu, and Kevin Gimpel. 2017. Pay attention to the ending: Strong neural baselines for the ROC Story Cloze Task. In *Proceedings of the 55th Annual Meeting of the Association for Computational Linguistics (Volume 2: Short Papers)*. Association for Computational Linguistics, pages 616–622.

Danqi Chen, Jason Bolton, and Christopher D. Manning. 2016. A thorough examination of the CNN/Daily Mail reading comprehension task. In *Association for Computational Linguistics (ACL)*.

Kyunghyun Cho, Bart van Merriënboer, Dzmitry Bahdanau, and Yoshua Bengio. 2014. On the properties of neural machine translation: Encoder–decoder approaches. *Syntax, Semantics and Structure in Statistical Translation* page 103.

Kenneth Ward Church and Patrick Hanks. 1990. Word association norms, mutual information, and lexicography. *Computational linguistics* 16(1):22–29.

Natalie Dehn. 1981. Story Generation After TALE-SPIN. *Proceedings of the 7th International Joint Conference on Artificial Intelligence (IJCAI '81)* pages 16–18.

Marjan Ghazvininejad, Xing Shi, Yejin Choi, and Kevin Knight. 2016. Generating topical poetry. In *EMNLP*. pages 1183–1191.

Andrew Gordon, Cosmin Adrian Bejan, and Kenji Sagae. 2011. Commonsense Causal Reasoning Using Millions of Personal Stories. *Twenty-Fifth Conference on Artificial Intelligence (AAAI-11)* pages 1180–1185.

Ting-Hao K. Huang, Francis Ferraro, Nasrin Mostafazadeh, Ishan Misra, Jacob Devlin, Aishwarya Agrawal, Ross Girshick, Xiaodong He, Pushmeet Kohli, Dhruv Batra, et al. 2016. Visual storytelling. In *15th Annual Conference of the North American Chapter of the Association for Computational Linguistics (NAACL 2016)*.

Diederik Kingma and Jimmy Ba. 2015. Adam: A method for stochastic optimization. In *The International Conference on Learning Representations (ICLR)*. San Diego.

Ryan Kiros, Yukun Zhu, Ruslan R Salakhutdinov, Richard Zemel, Raquel Urtasun, Antonio Torralba, and Sanja Fidler. 2015. Skip-thought vectors. In C. Cortes, N. D. Lawrence, D. D. Lee, M. Sugiyama, and R. Garnett, editors, *Advances in Neural Information Processing Systems 28*. Curran Associates, Inc., pages 3294–3302.

Michael Lebowitz. 1985. Story-telling as planning and learning. *Poetics* 14(6):483–502.

Boyang Li, Stephen Lee-Urban, George Johnston, and Mark Riedl. 2013. Story Generation with Crowd-sourced Plot Graphs. In *27th AAAI Conference on Artificial Intelligence*.

Zhiyi Luo, Yuchen Sha, Kenny Q. Zhu, Seung-won Hwang, and Zhongyuan Wang. 2016. Common-sense causal reasoning between short texts. In *15th International Conference on Principles of Knowledge Representation and Reasoning (KR-2016)*.

James R Meehan. 1977. TALE-SPIN, An Interactive Program that Writes Stories. In *5th International Joint Conference on Artificial Intelligence*. pages 91–98.

Tomas Mikolov, Ilya Sutskever, Kai Chen, Greg S Corrado, and Jeff Dean. 2013. Distributed representations of words and phrases and their compositionality. In *Advances in neural information processing systems*. pages 3111–3119.

Nasrin Mostafazadeh, Nathanael Chambers, Xiaodong He, Devi Parikh, Dhruv Batra, Lucy Vanderwende, Pushmeet Kohli, and James Allen. 2016. A corpus and cloze evaluation for deeper understanding of commonsense stories. In *Proceedings of NAACL-HLT*. pages 839–849.

Jeffrey Pennington, Richard Socher, and Christopher D. Manning. 2014. Glove: Global vectors for word representation. In *Empirical Methods in Natural Language Processing (EMNLP)*. pages 1532–1543.

Melissa Roemmele, Cosmin Adrian Bejan, and Andrew S. Gordon. 2011. Choice of Plausible Alternatives : An Evaluation of Commonsense Causal Reasoning. *AAAI Spring Symposium: Logical Formalizations of Commonsense Reasoning* pages 90–95.

Shota Sasaki, Sho Takase, Naoya Inoue, Naoaki Okazaki, and Kentaro Inui. 2017. Handling multi-word expressions in causality estimation. In *IWCS 201712th International Conference on Computational SemanticsShort papers*.

Roger C Schank and Robert P Abelson. 1977. *Scripts, plans, goals, and understanding: An inquiry into human knowledge structures*. Psychology Press.

Roger C Schank and Robert P Ableson. 1995. Knowledge and memory: The real story. *In. Rober S. Wyer (Ed.), Knowledge and memory: The real story* pages 1–85.

Abigail See, Peter J Liu, and Christopher D Manning. 2017. Get to the point: Summarization with pointer-generator networks. In *Association for Computational Linguistics (ACL)*.

Iulian Vlad Serban, Alessandro Sordoni, Yoshua Bengio, Aaron C Courville, and Joelle Pineau. 2016. Building end-to-end dialogue systems using generative hierarchical neural network models. In *AAAI*. pages 3776–3784.

Lifeng Shang, Zhengdong Lu, and Hang Li. 2015. Neural Responding Machine for Short-Text Conversation. In *Proceedings of the 53th Annual Meeting of Association for Computational Linguistics and the 7th International Joint Conference on Natural Language Processing (ACL-IJCNLP'15)*. pages 1577–1586.

Shashank Srivastava, Snigdha Chaturvedi, and Tom M Mitchell. 2016. Inferring interpersonal relations in narrative summaries. In *AAAI*. pages 2807–2813.

Qixin Wang, Tianyi Luo, Dong Wang, and Chao Xing. 2016. Chinese song iambics generation with neural attention-based model. In *Proceedings of the Twenty-Fifth International Joint Conference on Artificial Intelligence (IJCAI-16)*. pages 2943–2949.

Neural Events Extraction from Movie Descriptions

Alex Tozzo, Dejan Jovanović and Mohamed R. Amer
SRI International
201 Washington Rd
Princeton, NJ08540, USA
`{dejan.jovanovic, mohamed.amer}@sri.com`

Abstract

We present a novel approach for event extraction and abstraction from movie descriptions. Our event frame consists of 'who", "did what" "to whom", "where", and "when". We formulate our problem using a recurrent neural network, enhanced with structural features extracted from syntactic parser, and trained using curriculum learning by progressively increasing the difficulty of the sentences. Our model serves as an intermediate step towards question answering systems, visual storytelling, and story completion tasks. We evaluate our approach on MovieQA dataset.

1 Introduction

Understanding events is important to understanding a narrative. Event complexity varies from one story to another and the ability to extract and abstract them is essential for multiple applications. For question answering systems, a question narrows the scope of events to examine for an answer. For storytelling, events build an image in the reader's mind and constructs a storyline.

For event extraction, we apply Natural Language Processing (NLP) techniques to construct an event frame consisting of: "who", "did what" "to whom", "where", and "when". The more complex questions of "how" and "why" requires significantly more reasoning and beyond this paper's scope. Most syntactic NLP parsers, such as CoreNLP (Manning et al., 2014) and NLTK (Bird et al., 2009), focused on examining characteristics of the words, grammatical structure, word order, and meaning (Chomsky, 1957). On the other hand neural NLP approaches, such as SLING (Ringgaard et al., 2017) relies on large corpora to train such models in addition multiple knowledge databases. These approaches perform event extraction without context (often visual) of a movie or a movie script. When performing event extraction in relation to events in a story, the context can be gleaned from descriptions of the set or characters or prior events in a sequence. Additionally, we intend to develop an event extraction framework for a mixed-initiative, human-computer, system and intend to generate a human-readable event structure for user interaction.

In departure from syntactic approaches, we propose a hybrid, neural and symbolic, approach to address this problem. We benefit from both neural and symbolic formulations to extract events from movie text. Neural networks have been successfully applied to NLP problems, specifically, sequence-to-sequence or (sequence-to-vector) models (Sutskever et al., 2014) applied to machine translation and word-to-vector (Mikolov et al., 2013a). Here, we combine those approaches with supplemental structural information, specifically sentence length. Our approach models local information and global sentence structure.

For our training paradigm, we explored curriculum learning ((Bengio et al., 2009). To the best of our knowledge, we are the first to apply it to event extraction. Curriculum learning proposes a model can learn to perform better on a difficult task if it is first presented with easier training examples. Generally, in prior curriculum learning work, the final model attains a higher performance than if it were trained on the most difficult task from the start. In this work, we base the curriculum on sentence length, reasoning that shorter sentences have a simpler structure. Other difficulty metrics such as average word length, longest word length, and FleschKincaid readability score were not considered in this experiment, but may be considered for future work.

Instead of treating the sentence-to-event problem as a complete black-box putting the burden

Proceedings of the First Workshop on Storytelling, pages 60–66
New Orleans, Louisiana, June 5, 2018. ©2018 Association for Computational Linguistics

on the deep learning model, we simplify the problem by adding structure to the output sentence following the event frame structure, where some of the components could be present or absent. Furthermore, some sentences could contain multiple events. Weak labels were extracted from each sentence using the predicate as an anchor. We use structure rather than a bag-of-words because it encodes information about the relationships between words.

Our contributions are three-fold:
- New formulation for event extraction in movie descriptions.
- A curriculum learning framework for difficulty based learning.
- Benchmarking symbolic and neural approaches on MovieQA dataset.

The paper is organized as follows: section 2 reviews prior work; Section 3 formulates our approach; Section 4 specifies the learning framework; Section 5 presents our experiments; Section 6 describes our future work and conclusion.

2 Prior Work

Event extraction is a well established research problem in NLP. Parsers have been developed to extract events and event structures using a variety of methods both supervised and unsupervised.

(McClosky et al., 2011) uses dependency parsing to extract events from sentences (converted to a dependency tree by a separate classifier) by identifying event anchors in a sentence and graphing relationships to its arguments.

(Chambers and Jurafsky, 2008) and (Chambers and Jurafsky, 2009) develop an unsupervised method to learn narrative relations between events that share a co-reference argument and, later, a sequence of events over multiple sentences.

(Martin et al., 2017) and (Martin et al., 2018) present a neural technique for generating a mid-level event abstraction that retains the semantic information of the original sentence while minimizing event sparsity. They formulate the problem as first, the generation of successive events (event2event in their parlance), then generate natural language from events (event2sentence). The authors use a 4-tuple event representation with subject, verb, object, and a modifier of the sentence including prepositional phrase, indirect object, or causal complement. One key concept is that these events are in generalized Word-Net forms and are not easily human-readable. Their event2event network is an encoder-decoder model. The event2sentence model is similar to the event2event model with the exception of using beam search.

(Harrison et al., 2017) introduces a Monte Carlo approach for story generation, a related application of event extraction. Citing RNN's difficulty in maintaining coherence across multiple sentences, they develop a Markov Chain Monte Carlo model that can generate arbitrarily long sentences. In this work, they use the same event representation as (Martin et al., 2018).

Prior work in curriculum learning ((Bengio et al., 2009)) explored shape recognition and language modeling. Specifically for language modeling, they experiment with a model to predict the best word following a context of prior words in a correct English sentence. Their language modeling experiment expanded the vocabulary, increasing the task difficulty as more words were added to the corpus. More recent work ((Graves et al., 2017)) applied curriculum learning to question-answering problems on the bAbI dataset (Weston et al., 2015), designed to probe reasoning capabilities of machine learning systems.

The problem with symbolic approaches is the rigidity of the parsers and only basing the parses on the encoded knowledge. The neural approaches are unbounded and produce a huge variety of generated sentences. However, they are not conditioned on specific text and the results vary, often producing unrealistic sentences. We propose a hybrid of the two approaches to provide structured events conditioned on realistic content.

3 Approach

Our goal is to extract event frames in movie description in the format of "who" "did what" "to whom or what" "when" and "where". By extracting particular components of an event, it becomes easier to instantiate an event as an animation using existing software or present the event object to a human user for them to instantiate on their own terms. Once events are extracted in this format, a sequence of events can be used to animate the script and generate a short movie. In contrast to the purely symbolic approach taken by others, we take a neural approach, applying Recurrent Neural Networks (RNN). The idea is that an RNN will learn to output a structure mirroring the symbolic

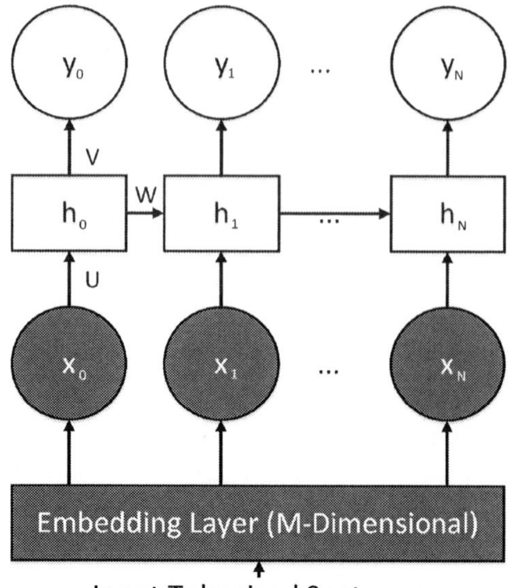

Figure 1: The model takes input word2vec vectors of each word and outputs their labels.

approaches. The input nodes are encoded as a fixed sequence of identical length and the output are labels of the provided structure. Figure 1 illustrates our model. We first encode each word in the input sentence to an M-dimensional vector using word2vec (Mikolov et al., 2013b). The embedding output vectors input an M-dimensional RNN with LSTM units. We standardized the length of the sentence by padding short sentences and capping the length of the longest sentence to be 25 words. The hidden state of each unit is defined in (1) for $h^{(t)}$. The output of each unit is $o^{(t)}$ and is equal to the hidden state. The internal cell state is defined by C^t. Intermediate variables $f^{(t)}$, $i^{(t)}$, $\hat{c}^{(t)}$, and $u^{(t)}$ facilitate readability and correspond to forget, input, and candidate gates, respectively. The cell state and the hidden state are propagated forwards in time to the next LSTM unit.

$$
\begin{aligned}
f^{(t)} &= \sigma(W_{fh}h^{(t-1)} + W_{fx}x^{(t)} + b_f) \\
\hat{c}^{(t)} &= \tanh(W_{ch}h^{(t-1)} + W_{cx}x^{(t)} + b_c) \\
i^{(t)} &= \sigma(W_{ih}h^{(t-1)} + W_{ix}x^{(t)} + b_i) \\
C^{(t)} &= C^{(t-1)} \odot f^{(t)} + i^{(t)} \odot \hat{c}^{(t)} \\
o^{(t)} &= \sigma(W_{oh}h^{(t-1)} + W_{ox}x^{(t)} + b_o) \\
h^{(t)} &= \tanh(C^{(t)}) \odot o^{(t)}
\end{aligned}
\tag{1}
$$

A significant hurdle in training any of network in this instance is class imbalance. Here, the model is trained using standard back-propagation with a weighted cross-entropy loss function used to avoid over-fitting to the null class.

4 Curriculum Learning

Sentences vary in difficulty due to structure, context, vocabulary, and more. As part of our experiments, we employed curriculum learning to potentially facilitate the learning processes. We compare the curriculum training to standard batch processing.

We divide the training samples into three difficulty groups based on sentence length. We train the model with the easiest set first for 100 epochs before advancing to the medium and hard difficulty training samples, training for 100 epochs each. This results in 300 training epochs total, although the model is only exposed to a third of the dataset for 100 epochs at a time. We compare this to models where the training process exposes the model to the entire corpus for 300 epochs. We use sentence length, assuming that shorter sentences are easier as they contain fewer descriptive words, but other structural and semantic metrics can be used.

5 Experiments

MovieQA Dataset (Tapaswi et al., 2016): We use the descriptive video service (DVS) text from MovieQA. The DVS sentences tend to be simpler and describe the scene explicitly compared to the plot synopsis sentences. We generate an initial training corpus of extracted events using dependency parsers and information extraction annotators from CoreNLP. A total of 36,898 events are generated. Analyzing the corpus of extracted events, we found the longest sentence length contained 62 words. However, by limiting our dataset to sentences with 25 words or less, we retained 97% of the data (35791 sentences). Figure 3 shows the sentence length distribution of the DVS data and the plot synopsis data. We did not experiment with the plot synopsis data, rather we wish to highlight the difference in sentence lengths between the 2 sets of data. The DVS data is heavily skewed towards shorter sentences, most likely due to requiring concise descriptions about what is happening on screen at that time. Plot synopsis sentences tend to be longer as they tend to summarize multiple actions and plot points. Sentences with multiple predicates generated multiple events and this manifested itself as duplicate sentences in our dataset with multiple label sequences. Sentences with multiple events accounted for about 24% of the data. This does lead to complications for train-

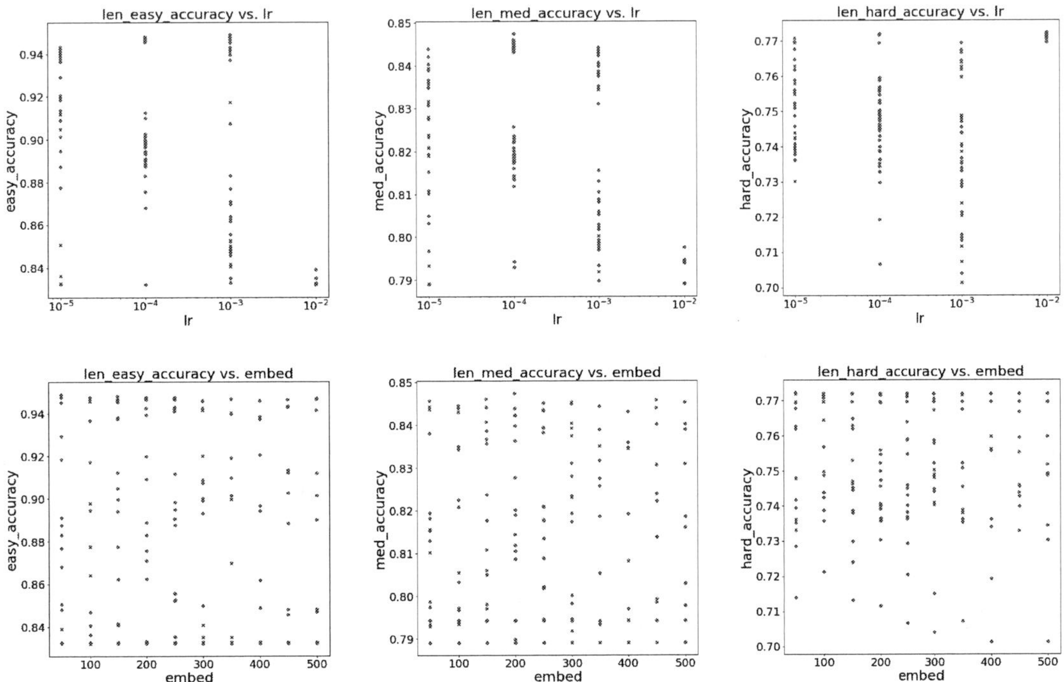

Figure 2: (Top, left to right) Easy, Medium, Hard Accuracy vs Learning Rate. (Bottom, left to right) Easy, Medium, Hard Accuracy vs Embedding Dimension.

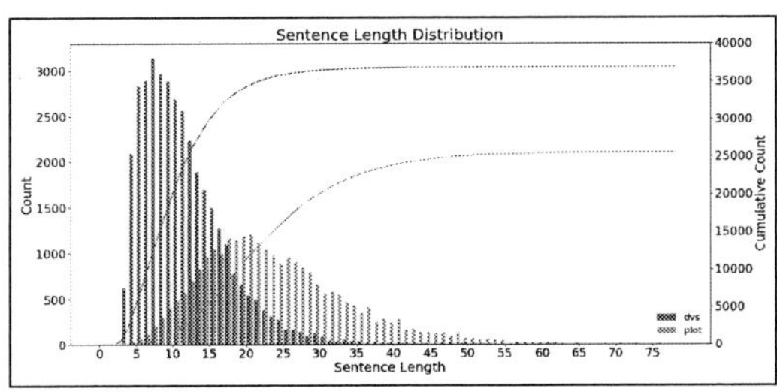

Figure 3: Sentence Length Distribution from DVS (blue) and Plot Synopsis (orange) Data and Cumulative Distribution (solid lines and right axis)

ing as we did not distinguish between events.

The difficulty classes computed by sentence length and are as follows: easy sentences are 8 words or less with an average sentence length of 6.5 words, medium sentences are 9-12 words with an average length of 10.4 words, and hard sentences are 13 words or longer with an average length of 16.8 words. Each difficulty class is contains one third of the original data set. For training with and without a curriculum, we used an 80-20 train-test split. For curriculum learning, each difficulty was trained on 80% of each of the respective difficulty sets and tested on the remaining 20%.

The extracted events provide weak labels generated by the CoreNLP algorithm approach.

Pre-processing: We tokenized the text assigning an integer to each word after removing capitalization and apostrophes. Sentences are vectorized using this index. The output format assigns integers between 1-5 to parts of the sentence based on which elements of the sentence are part of the subject (1), predicate (2), object (3), location (4), or time (5) phrases. Articles, prepositions, conjunctions, adjectives, and adverbs were often assigned the null class (0) although some may be included parts of event phrases. Sentences are left-padded with zeros make all sentence vectors the same length.

Implementation Details: The trained model is a basic LSTM model. We employ two different training approaches. In the first approach, we ignore the sentence length and use random batches of training data. We train for 300 epochs. Second, we use a training curriculum based on sentence length, starting training with shorter sentences and progressing to longer sentences. The sentences are divided into easy, medium, and hard difficulty sets with each set containing roughly one-third of the

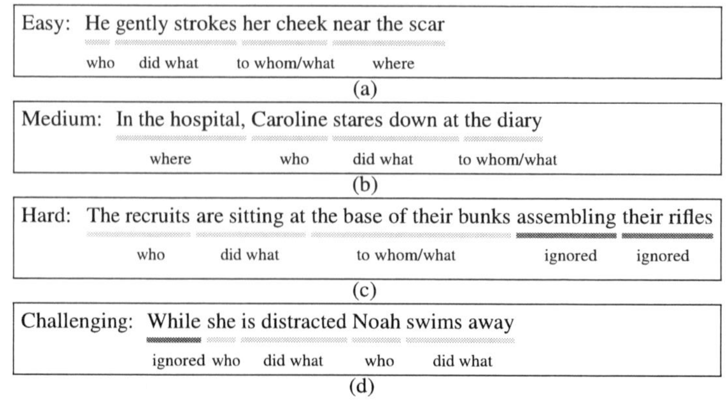

Figure 4: Successful Cases

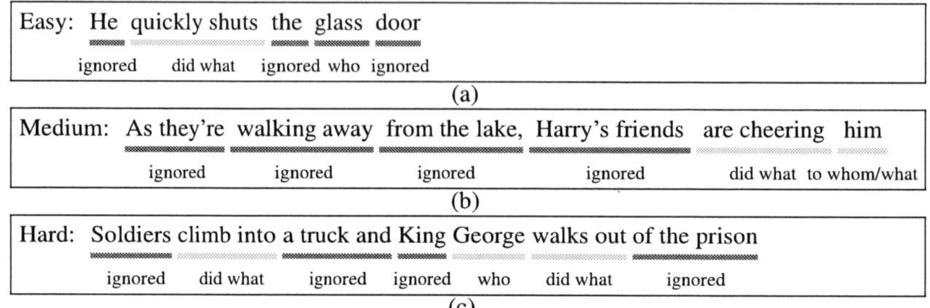

Figure 5: Failure Cases

total data set. We hold out a set of data from each difficulty level for validation. We train the model for 100 epochs on each level of difficulty to match the total of 300 epochs of the random training curriculum. The final approach is to start with shorter sentence lengths and train with longer sentences towards the end.

We examine four parameters: the learning rate, the embedding dimension, the hidden dimension, and number of training epochs. A grid search was employed to examine the effects of these parameters on the validation accuracy. We varied learning rate in powers of 10 from $1e - 5$ to $1e - 2$. The embedding dimension was varied from 50-500 in increments of 50. The hidden dimension was varied from 48-512 in increments of 16. Lastly, we varied the number of training epochs from 300-2000 in increments of 200. Below we include a sample of figures from this search where we fixed the number of epochs (300) and the hidden layer dimension (512) while adjusting the learning rate and the embedding dimension. For these parameters, we found an embedding dimension of 350 performs best on the easy and medium difficulty levels. Additional training is in progress.

We used ADAM (Kingma and Ba, 2014) for gradient optimization. Our loss function was a weighted categorical cross entropy function using the class distribution from the training data as class weights. Accuracy is calculated by the frequency with which the predicted class matches the labels. The accuracy is then the total count of actual matches by the total potential matches.

5.1   Qualitative Results

In this work, we used the symbolic algorithm as a weak label for the neural network approach. The symbolic approach appears to work well for shorter sentences with simple sentence structure. However, as the sentences become longer and additional descriptive phrases, the dependency parsing becomes more complex. We present 3 examples (1 from each difficulty level) of a simple sentence the symbolic algorithm does well.

Figure 4 shows examples where our approach was successful. Figure 4(a) illustrates an easy difficulty sentence. The parser correctly identifies the *he* as the subject, *gently strokes* as the verb phrase, *her cheek* as the object, and *near the scar* as the location. Figure 4(b) illustrates a medium difficulty sentence. The parser identifies *Caroline* as the subject again, the verb phrase *stares down at*, the object *diary* and the location *in the hos-*

pital. Figure 4(b) illustrates a medium difficulty sentence. Figure 4(c) illustrates a hard difficulty sentence. The parser identifies *recruits* as the subject. The verb phrase identified here is *are sitting at* and the object is *base of their bunks*. Another verb phrase that could be identified is *assembling* with the object *their rifles*. These examples also show how the model ignored articles in the sentences. Finally, Figure 4(d) illustrates a challenging sentence. One pleasantly surprising example of the model learning multiple events in a single short sentence. The model correctly identifies 2 subjects (*she, Noah*) and 2 verb phrases (*is distracted, swims away*).

Figure 4 shows examples where our approach failed. Figure 5(a) illustrates an easy difficulty sentence. The model incorrectly identifies *glass* as a predicate while correctly identifying *shuts*, suggesting the model does not anchor events around a predicate phrase. Figure 5(b) illustrates an medium difficulty sentence. The model identifies the verb phrase *are cheering* and the object *him*, but fails to recognize the subject *Harry's friends*. This is odd as it would suggest the model doesn't recognize possessive apostrophes as part of a noun phrase, but may be confusing it with a contraction. However, other situations show the model does not recognize the contraction either. Figure 5(c) illustrates a hard difficulty sentence. The model fails to identify *soldiers* as a subject of any predicate, yet correctly identifies *climb into* and *walks out of* as predicate phrases. It does, however, identify *George* as a subject, but not his descriptor of *King*.

As sentences get longer, the model begins to breakdown. This may be due to the weak labels provided by the symbolic algorithm. It may also be due to the non-linear relationship between subject, predicate, and object in the sentence. The neural model also fails when the location is a generic place such as a *cafe* or *garage*. One improvement could be to incorporate the WordNet meaning of each word in the sentence.

5.2 Quantitative Results

We show results from curriculum learning using the sentence length as a basis for the curriculum. The accuracy is shown in Figure 6 for both the non-curriculum learning and the length-based curriculum. We first train with easy data, wit the easy validation data closely tracking it. After 200 epochs, we begin training with medium difficulty data. At this point, the easy validation data changes only a little, while medium and hard difficulty validation data continue to increase slightly. At 400 epochs, we begin training with the most difficult data: data containing the longest set of sentences our dataset. Introducing the hard training data affects the easy and medium validation accuracy. The hard difficulty validation accuracy continues to increase while easy and medium drop. Due to the semi-supervised method of labeling the data using symbolic methods, we believe longer sentences tend to be noisier and less accurately labeled compared to shorter sentences. This introduces noisy labels for the network, confusing it on previously learned examples leading to degraded performance. Descriptive phrases containing nouns can complicate the network and hinder identification of subject or object.

6   Conclusions and Future Work

This work presents an initial study of neural event extraction. We intend to study a bidirectional LSTMs and encoder-decoder models in future work. We anticipate bidirectional models and encoder-decoder models will enable the network to capture longer-term dependencies between object and predicate. We also plan to extend the data set to additional sources with human annotations for more accurate ground truth labels.

An additional direction for future work is to incorporate graphs as a mechanism to enforce structure. In addition, we can extract events from visual information and use it to guide the events extracted from textual information. Using graphs generated from both visual and textual information will result in a more complete, and less noisy event representation.

This experiment is a component for our work towards developing a mixed-initiative system for visual storytelling. Here, we take preliminary steps towards extracting events from movie descriptions with the intention of then instantiating events in an animation module. The simplified event structure facilitates the mixed system where either the computer or human can suggest events or render the event in a particular style or genre. Our vision for the system is to have a human and a computer take turns suggesting new events in a story or suggest a story arc and generate pertinent, relevant events to justify the conclusion.

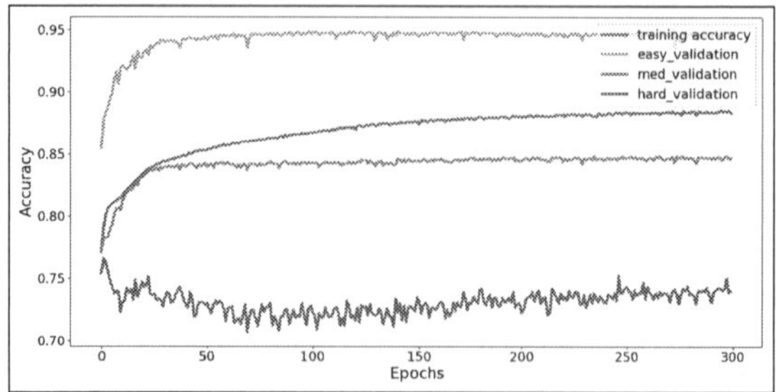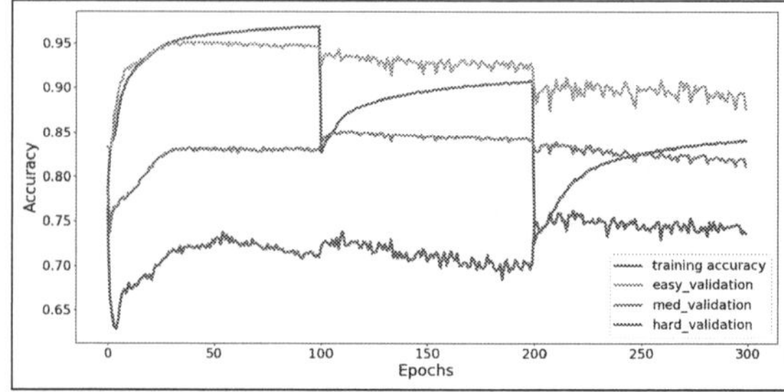

Figure 6: (Left) No curriculum learning with all difficulties mixed into training data. Validated against all difficulty levels at each epoch. (Right) Curriculum learning based on sentence length. Each difficulty trained for 100 epochs in easy, medium, hard order. Validated against all difficulty levels at each epoch.

Acknowledgments

This work is funded by DARPA W911NF-15-C-0246. The views, opinions, and/or conclusions contained in this paper are those of the author and should not be interpreted as representing the official views or policies, either expressed or implied of the DARPA or the DoD. Special thanks to Karine Megerdoomian for the helpful discussions.

References

Yoshua Bengio, Jrme Louradour, Ronan Collobert, and Jason Weston. 2009. Curriculum learning. *ICML*.

Steven Bird, Ewan Klein, and Edward Loper. 2009. *Natural Language Processing with Python*. OReilly Media Inc.

Nathanael Chambers and Dan Jurafsky. 2008. Unsupervised learning of narrative event chains. *ACL*.

Nathanael Chambers and Dan Jurafsky. 2009. Unsupervised learning of narrative schemas and their participants. *IJCNLP*.

N. Chomsky. 1957. Syntactic structures.

Alex Graves, Marc G. Bellemare, Jacob Menick, Remi Munos, and Koray Kavukcuoglu. 2017. Automated curriculum learning for neural networks. *ICML*.

Brent Harrison, Christopher Purdy, and Mark O. Riedl. 2017. Toward automated story generation with markov chain monte carlo methods and deep neural networks. In *Workshop on Intelligent Narrative Technologie*.

Diederik P. Kingma and Jimmy Ba. 2014. Adam: A method for stochastic optimization. *CoRR*, abs/1412.6980.

Christopher D. Manning, Mihai Surdeanu, John Bauer, Jenny Finkel, Steven J. Bethard, and David Mc-Closky. 2014. The Stanford CoreNLP natural language processing toolkit. In *ACL-Systems*.

Lara J. Martin, Prithviraj Ammanabrolu, Xinyu Wang, Shruti Singh, Brent Harrison, Pradyumna Tambwekar Murtaza Dhuliawala, Animesh Mehta, Richa Arora, Nathan Dass, Chris Purdy, and Mark O. Riedl. 2017. Improvisational storytelling agents. In *NIPS-Workshops*.

Lara J. Martin, Prithviraj Ammanabrolu, Xinyu Wang, Shruti Singh, Brent Harrison, and Mark O. Riedl. 2018. Event representations for automated story generation with deep neural nets. In *AAAI*.

David McClosky, Mihai Surdeneau, and Christopher D. Manning. 2011. Event extraction as dependency parsing. *Proceedings of BioNLP Shared Task 2011 Workshop*.

Tomas Mikolov, Kai Chen, Greg Corrado, and Jeffrey Dean. 2013a. Efficient estimation of word representations in vector space. *CoRR*, abs/1301.3781.

Tomas Mikolov, Kai Chen, Greg Corrado, and Jeffrey Dean. 2013b. Efficient estimation of word representations in vector space. *CoRR*, abs/1301.3781.

Michael Ringgaard, Rahul Gupta, and Fernando C. N. Pereira. 2017. SLING: A framework for frame semantic parsing. *CoRR*, abs/1710.07032.

Ilya Sutskever, Oriol Vinyals, and Quoc V. Le. 2014. Sequence to sequence learning with neural networks. *CoRR*, abs/1409.3215.

Makarand Tapaswi, Yukun Zhu, Rainer Stiefelhagen, Antonio Torralba, Raquel Urtasun, and Sanja Fidler. 2016. Movieqa: Understanding stories in movies through question-answering. In *IEEE Conference on Computer Vision and Pattern Recognition (CVPR)*.

Jason Weston, Antoine Bordes, Sumit Chopra, and Tomas Mikolov. 2015. Towards ai-complete question answering: A set of prerequisite toy tasks. *CoRR*, abs/1502.05698.

Author Index

Association for Computational Linguistics
209 N. Eighth Street
Stroudsburg, Pennsylvania 18360

ISBN 978-1-5108-6365-1